CW00798324

Do Police Need Guns?

Richard Evans · Clare Farmer

Do Police Need Guns?

Policing and Firearms: Past, Present and Future

 Springer

Richard Evans
School of Humanities and Social Sciences
Deakin University
Geelong, Australia

Clare Farmer
School of Humanities and Social Sciences
Deakin University
Geelong, Australia

ISBN 978-981-15-9525-7   ISBN 978-981-15-9526-4   (eBook)
https://doi.org/10.1007/978-981-15-9526-4

This Springer imprint is published by the registered company Springer Nature Singapore Pte Ltd.
The registered company address is: 152 Beach Road, #21-01/04 Gateway East, Singapore 189721, Singapore

Foreword

In November 2019, two police officers attended a property in Yuendumu, 300 km north-west of Alice Springs in the Northern Territory of Australia to arrest a man for an alleged breach of a condition of his suspended sentence. A confrontation occurred. Hostile words were exchanged. A shot was fired, and a nineteen-year-old Aboriginal man lay dying.

In Australia, on average, around seven persons are killed by police firearms each year. Why is this still happening? Surely police have learned lessons from past tragedies? Are not police trained today to use their guns only as a last resort? These questions and many more are addressed in this new and important book. By exploring the theory and practice of arming police and comparing hard data on police and community safety in four different nations, this book begins an essential conversation, one which is relevant to communities across the world.

Does the routine arming of police make them safer? The evidence suggests that there is no difference to the vulnerability of law enforcement officers in those jurisdictions that do not have routine carriage. However, armed officers report that they feel safer.

Does the routine arming of police make the public safer? The literature tells us that the number of civilian deaths caused by police firearms varies according to four important factors: the extent of police militarisation, the gun culture in the society in which officers operate, the rules that pertain to the use of lethal force and the standards of firearm training.

The answers to such questions are important for policy development. Arguably, the most significant considerations for policymakers in jurisdictions where police are routinely armed are the last two: rules and training. To that end, there are a number of imperatives that emerge from the research. Police policies across all jurisdictions require clear and precise rules regarding the carriage and drawing of firearms, and high standards of accountability for those who carry or draw. There must be uniform and regular firearm training. This training must include best practice communication techniques, negotiation skills and de-escalation strategies, and clear instructions regarding the deployment of non-lethal alternatives. Research highlights the benefits of body cameras on operational officers, too, as a means of encouraging alternative strategies. Finally, training must also include developing collaborative engagements with health professionals and allied community services.

If these initiatives and practices are in place, and entrenched, one can safely assert that fewer deaths at the hands of police will occur.

The authors lead their readers through the paths of practice that best balance personal safety and public security. They ask important questions about the routine arming of police; they explore the research; they review the evidence; they consider the alternatives. I am grateful that Richard Evans and Clare Farmer have made it easier for us to navigate this difficult road.

Emeritus Professor Rick Sarre
University of South Australia
Adelaide, Australia

Acknowledgements

We extend our thanks to Victoria Police for granting permission to use images from *Police Life* magazine in this book. We also thank the School of Humanities and Social Sciences at Deakin University, and Strategic Data Pty Ltd.

Contents

Key Terminology

Exploring basic questions about policing, the use of force and firearms presents linguistic challenges. For example, are the police a "force" or a "service"? The two terms are in common use, but in the context of this book are loaded with implication. We have endeavoured to be both clear and consistent, sometimes at the expense of elegant writing. When discussing policing organisations in general, we refrain from using the terms "police force" or "police service". Where the context requires, we use the term "police organisation"; where there is no danger of confusion, the simple term "police" is used.

Another problematic area is members of the public who are killed by police. Many policing texts refer to these people as "felons" or "offenders", an assertion of guilt and culpability which is not always justified and which we specifically reject. The term "civilian" is also used, but this is a borrowing from the language of warfare and describes a non-combatant. The implication is that police face rival combatants (presumably offenders) who can legitimately be targeted for the use of lethal force in a way which would not be allowed for "civilians". Other possibilities are "citizen" (unsatisfactory because non-citizens are also part of the policed community), and "member of the public", which is correct but clumsy. With some reluctance we have chosen to use the term "civilian", however we emphasise that this applies to all non-police. In using force, police have a duty of care which extends to and includes dangerous criminal offenders: these are also "civilians", whether or not the use of lethal force was necessary or justified.

In theoretical discussions of power and society, it is useful to refer to the State, meaning the combined organisational and legal apparatus which forms official authority in a modern community, and of which the police is one facet. However, states are also jurisdictional units in both Australia and (obviously) the United States of America. In this book, we use "State" with a capital letter in the general and abstract sense. For political, governmental entities, such as the Australian states of Queensland or Victoria, lower case is used.

A political entity which is famously confusing is the United Kingdom of Great Britain and Northern Ireland, usually referred to as the United Kingdom or Britain. When referring to the whole nation, we will use the term United Kingdom (UK).

The UK comprises four nations: England, Wales, Scotland and Northern Ireland. However, England and Wales form a unitary jurisdiction from policing perspective and include the city of Manchester, one of the locations used in this study. Thus, it is necessary to use the slightly clumsy formulations "England/Wales" or "England and Wales" when discussing jurisdictions across our comparative study. The abbreviation EW is sometimes used in tables and figures.

Abbreviations

Auck   Auckland
Aus   Australia
Bri   Brisbane
Can   Canada
EW   England and Wales
Man   Manchester
NZ   New Zealand
Tor   Toronto

Chapter 1
Introduction

Abstract In the modern State, police are the sole agents of authorised violence. Many other agencies and services are vital to a society's well-being, but underpinning all of them is the police, who have both the right and the duty to use violence, up to and including lethal force, on behalf of the community as a whole. The use of force by police is one of the most important issues facing any community. You might then expect that there would be detailed and exhaustive studies of the police use of firearms, and the implications of arming police for the safety of police and the community. However, this is not the case. There is rhetoric aplenty, from both opponents of and advocates for routinely armed police, but almost no empirically informed evidence. In this introduction, we set the scene for the detailed exploration of the theory and practice of police use of force, and especially the use of firearms, which makes up this book. We outline the structure and briefly summarise each chapter, and also explain the "American paradox": why this book examines influential American models of policing, both in scholarship and popular culture, but does not contain a US case study.

1.1 Do Police Need Guns?

In the modern State, police are the sole agents of authorised violence. Many other agencies and services are vital to a society's well-being: schools and hospitals, sewerage and banking, media and law courts, the electricity grid and vehicle registration, and on and on. However, underpinning all of them is the police. The police mandate is to protect life and property, to preserve the peace, and to enforce the laws. These goals are complex and often in tension, and relative priorities are endlessly contested, particularly in response to social and political change. However, regardless of changes in focus and policy, a reasonably professional and disciplined police organisation is an essential feature of the modern State. And police have both the right and the duty to use violence, up to and including lethal force, on behalf of the community as a whole.

The use of force by police, then, is one of the most important issues facing any community. In what situations are police entitled to use force, against whom, and to what level? What theory of force should police use, going about their vital work, and what tools should they have at their disposal? All modern policing organisations subscribe to some form of the doctrine of minimum force. Put simply, police have the right to use force, but only when it is necessary, and then only to the minimum degree necessary.

The ultimate expression of State violence is the use of lethal force by police, and by far the most common tool used to inflict lethal force is a firearm. A police officer's gun then, also assumes enormous symbolic power. A gun worn by a police officer and visible to the public carries a message, a reminder: "this person can kill you". To the officer, it is a constant presence, a potential: "if I have to kill someone, I can". Visible firearms carried by police are, almost by their very nature, in tension with the doctrine of minimum force.

Over the past forty years, across the developed world, policing has steadily, consistently become more reliant on firearms as both as tool and symbol of police power. In those jurisdictions where police are routinely armed, the firearms carried have become more visible, more numerous and more powerful. In those jurisdictions where police are not routinely armed, pressure is building for firearms to be carried on routine patrol. The justification for this move is invariably rooted in the idea of safety. Police need routine access to weapons, or more powerful weapons than they already carry, both so they can protect the community, and to ensure their own safety.

Given that the use of force by police is so important and so contentious, you might expect that there would be detailed and exhaustive study of the police use of firearms, and the implications of arming police for the safety of police and the community. However, this is not the case. There is rhetoric aplenty, from both opponents of and advocates for routinely armed police: aphoristic statements, the repetition of received wisdom, war stories and anecdotes, but almost no empirically informed evidence.

This book has its origins in a comparative study written in cooperation with a colleague, which explored the nexus between mental illness and gun violence in the United States, Australia and Great Britain (Evans et al. 2016).

We concluded that only different levels of access to firearms could explain the different rates of gun deaths, whether perpetrated by offenders or police.

> In the UK, guns are difficult to obtain and the police are not usually armed. A person suffering a mental health crisis is unlikely to be able to cause serious harm to other people, and the police will almost always be able to resolve such a crisis without a fatality. In Australia, guns are difficult to obtain but the police are routinely armed. The greatest risk of fatality is for the mentally ill person, due to a police response which automatically involves firearms. In the US, firearms are very readily accessible. A mentally ill person in crisis often has a weapon available capable of easily inflicting lethal violence, in some cases upon a large number of people in a short time. Police are also usually armed, and although the data is unsatisfactory an unknown (but probably large) proportion of an unknown (but very large) number of civilians shot dead are mentally ill.

> The fewer guns there are in a community, whether in the hands of civilians or of police, the safer that community is (Evans et al. 2016: 156).

This last statement begs a question. The community might be demonstrably safer where police are not routinely armed—but what about police themselves?

In our home country, Australia, criticism of police use of firearms tends to come from scholars and commentators who are socially and politically progressive, and suspicious of police violence. They draw attention to the disproportionate numbers of people killed or injured by police, who belong to already marginalised and disadvantaged communities. Police reaction to such criticism tends to be defensive, and framed in terms of police safety: policing is difficult and dangerous, and while tragic accidents occur and are regrettable, we need to carry firearms to do our jobs. This argument carries great weight with governments, and Australia's police remain routinely-armed. While the details of such discussion vary between jurisdictions, the broad outline will be wearily familiar to any student of policing.

Our hope, in this book, is to elevate discussions of policing and firearms beyond this set-piece exchange.

Deaths in the community caused by police firearms, particularly when those killed are vulnerable, is a legitimate concern.

The safety of police officers is a legitimate concern.

What does the evidence from the real world tell us about these fundamental and important aspects of policing? This book documents our comparative study of four locations, two where police are routinely armed and two where police are not routinely armed. The purpose of the study is to start the process of gathering real-world, demonstrable evidence to examine the effect on safety of routinely arming police officers. The rationale for the study, the research design and findings are set out in Chaps. 5 and 6.

We have framed our comparative study by first exploring basic questions about the nature of police power (Chap. 2). We then examine the origins, theoretical underpinnings and evolution of different philosophies of policing; in Chap. 3 we consider minimum force policing, and in Chap. 4 we document the armed tradition of policing, and the steady move towards increased police militarisation. In light of the findings of our examination of four jurisdictions, in Chap. 7 we reflect upon the influence of media texts and popular culture on perceptions of policing and firearms to consider from where the continued belief in the need for routinely armed policing may derive.

"Do police need guns?" is a provocative question, but it is a completely serious question. Whatever answer our communities decide on, that answer should be based on a sound and coherent theory of policing and power, and clear demonstrable evidence from the real world. We hope that this book represents a beginning to a process which encourages and supports a more thoughtful and better-evidenced discussion of firearms and the role that they play in policing.

1.2 The American Paradox

In this book, we explore two contrasting approaches to policing, and examine the role of firearms in each. One approach we call the minimum force doctrine (see Chap. 3), a tradition which is exemplified in one of our case studies: Manchester, England. The other approach we call the armed tradition (see Chap. 4), and we identify it firmly with the history and contemporary influence of the United States.

It may seem strange, then, that we do not include the United States or one of its cities in our comparative study (see Chaps. 5 and 6). If American models are so dominant, surely an American city should be part of this research? That was, in fact, our initial expectation. We examined cities of suitable size and population in the United States, intending to include one as a case study. There are several locations with roughly the right population and regional status, including Chicago, Illinois (2.7 million people) and San Antonio, Texas (1.6 million). Another Texas city, Houston (2.4 million) was considered in some detail. It became plain, however, that a meaningful comparative study which included a US city would be almost impossible.

Several external variables affect the compatibility of our four chosen locations and already represent a challenge to this study (see Chap. 5). Examples include differences in local law, the make-up of migrant communities, forms of police governance, and rates of serious crime. These challenges are multiplied greatly in a US context.

The most obvious problems are differences in attitudes to, laws governing, and rates of civilian gun ownership. Consider the cases of Brisbane, Australia, and Houston. Brisbane has a population of 2.2 million, similar to Houston. Based on rates of gun ownership, there would be roughly 260,000 registered civilian firearms in Brisbane (University of Sydney 2019). The exact figure would be lower, because a high proportion of civilian firearms in Australia are owned by farmers and other rural residents, rather than people in cities (McPhedran 2014). Of these weapons, only about 16,000 would be handguns, as personal protection is specifically excluded as a justification for gun ownership (Queensland Police 2020). None of these weapons would be semi-automatic, military grade rifles, which are banned. There would, of course, also be an unknown number of illegally owned firearms. By contrast, in the slightly larger city of Houston, there would be roughly 2.9 million registered firearms (Karp 2018: 4). A large proportion of these weapons would be handguns and powerful semi-automatic rifles. The dark figure of illegally held firearms in Houston is also unknown but would certainly be substantial.

In such contrasting environments, the role and use of firearms by police present enormous difficulties for a comparative study. The locations used in our study have been selected to be as homogeneous as possible. The inclusion of a US city such as Houston would significantly skew the analysis.

There are other complicating factors. In the United States, the quality of available data is often poor. Even such basic quanta as the number of fatalities caused by police shootings are either not available, or notoriously unreliable (see Chap. 4). Another difficulty is the historic role of police in the subjugation of black slaves. The jurisdictions we examine all share experiences of police racism and discrimination towards particular population groups. However, in none of them was there a centuries-long experience of industrial-scale slavery across large parts of the country. The legacy of slavery shapes American policing to this day, as is evident in the widespread protests against police racism and violence which are unfolding at the time of writing (in mid 2020). Racism certainly plays a role in police-community relations elsewhere, but the picture is different. Again, Houston or another US city would be an anomalous, complicating example which would compromise and complicate useful comparison.

This, then, is the American paradox. In terms of crime, risk and policing, America is a statistical "First-World outlier," and any comparison is further complicated by the complex legacy of large-scale slavery and a fragmented and uneven system of law enforcement statistics. However, American news media, popular culture and scholarship are all so dominant in the Anglophone world, including in all the locations we look at in this book, that it is impossible to ignore the American influence. America is both "another planet" in terms of policing, but also the single most important influence on policing in the rest of the Anglophone world. This book does not include a US comparative study, because comparison is so difficult. On the other hand, we cannot ignore US influence, as it shapes understanding and policy in the jurisdictions we consider.

References

Evans, R., Farmer, C., & Saligari, J. (2016). Mental illness and gun violence: Lessons for the United States from Australia and Britain. *Violence & Gender, 3*(3), 150–156.

Karp, A. (2018). *Estimating global civilian-held firearms numbers*. Geneva: Small Arms Survey.

McPhedran, S. (2014). Does rural Australia have a gun problem? *The Conversation*, 28 Oct.

Queensland Police. (2020). *Weapons licensing* [online]. Available from: https://www.police.qld.gov.au/knowledge-centre?combine=&weapon_licensing_type%5B15%5D=15. Accessed 17 Aug 2020.

University of Sydney. (2019). *GunPolicy.org* [online]. University of Sydney. Available from: https://www.gunpolicy.org/about. Accessed 17 Aug 2020.

Chapter 2
The Edge of the Knife: The Paradox of Police Power

Abstract As is true of power more generally, the power of police is an under-researched and under-theorised aspect of society. Most policing textbooks evade the question of what constitutes police power, instead creating a brief narrative arc, one of rationalist progress from semi-mythologised origins to contemporary legal and administrative structures. The extensive critique of policing in capitalist society from a Marxist perspective, which situates policing as an expression of the violence which is fundamental to capitalism, is acknowledged. However, we criticise as a major weakness the "implied alternative": a social formation which does not rely on violence or the threat of violence. We argue that all societies are underpinned by violence; that all societies have policing in some form; and that large, complex modern societies require a reasonably professional and disciplined police organisation to function. This is the consequence of the Hobbesian social contract: individual citizens surrender their rights to use violence in return for the protection of the State. The benefits of this arrangement can be explained by borrowing Talcott Parson's "monetary model" of power. By this view, police power is analogous to a fiscal system: the "power banks" of the State, of which the police are the most important, allow people to use power which is not their own. Like a fiscal system, police power too is dependent on public trust and confidence. This informs the notion of policing by consent, and the doctrine of minimum force which are explored in Chap. 3.

2.1 Introduction

In William Golding's book *Lord of the Flies*, a group of evacuee children are stranded on a remote island. Early in the novel Roger, later to become a figure of evil, observes a younger boy, Henry, playing at the water's edge.

> Roger gathered a handful of stones and began to throw them. Yet there was a space round Henry, perhaps six yards in diameter, into which he dare not throw. Here, invisible yet strong, was the taboo of the old life. Round the squatting child was the protection of parents and school and police men and the law …. (Golding 1960: 77)

Lord of the Flies is a story of original sin. Unrestrained by "parents and police", the group of children swiftly descend into chaos, violence and cruelty. In this passage, Golding touches on a core truth about police power. It is usually purely symbolic, "invisible yet strong," based on social habit and ways of thinking rather than any physical reality.

In this chapter, we apply a range of theoretical concepts regarding policing, State power and the use of force to examine what underpins police power. Specifically, we note the weakness of most conventional attempts to position policing as part of a "march of progress" narrative. We assess the Marxist critique of policing, and find that there is a fatal weakness in seeking to explain violence as a facet of the capitalist social order: put simply, violence is a facet of every conceivable social order. While policing is an ancient social function, professional and disciplined police are both a product of and necessary to large scale and complex modern societies. We argue that the most useful theory for understanding police is the monetary model proposed by Talcott Parsons. This sets the scene for a closer examination of the notion of policing by consent, and specifically the doctrine of minimum force, in Chap. 3.

2.2   What Makes the Police Powerful?

To answer the question "Do police need guns?" we first need to examine a more basic question: what makes the police powerful? That police, both as individuals and as an institution, have considerable power is obvious. The nature of that power, however, is elusive and paradoxical. The foundations of police power became a topic of scholarship in the late 1960s and early 1970s, as part of a response to the social upheaval then challenging established verities in the United States (US), the United Kingdom (UK) and many other societies (Milte and Weber 1977: 1–5). In 1972, Ramsay Clark, a former US Attorney-General, identified a lacunae at the heart of policing:

> Too often, when we are confronted with the necessity of stating the idea behind the most common and essential functions in society, we realise that we have no idea. We do the things we do mainly because we have done them before, adding new usages to old ones as our immediate needs change. So it is with civil police. Where among the great ideas do we find a clearly developed concept of civil police? … Where among the great books is there a significant treatment? (Clarke 1972: 5)

A similar need to rethink was identified in British policy circles. Sociologist Michael Chatterton challenged much of what was commonly understood about policing. "In everyday life we fail to realise that many of the things we refer to as *facts* are actually *beliefs*. Hence, ways of life and patterns of activity appear to be 'natural' and 'inevitable'" [original emphasis] (Chatterton 1973: 112). These ways of thinking, he argued, are often scarcely conscious. Precisely for that reason they are enormously powerful: "conduct norms we follow without thinking about them" can be of greater importance than formal rules such as the written law (Chatterton 1973: 112).

With some semi-exceptions (which are considered below), "a clearly developed concept of civil police" remains elusive. There has been a great deal of scholarship examining police *powers*, the law which guides and restrains what police are able lawfully to do, and this is important (See, for example, Dubber 2005; Jason-Lloyd 2005; Macleod and Schneiderman 1994; Stobbs 2009). There has also been analysis of how police actually use their power, whether that is legally enshrined, a matter of workplace custom, or even outright criminal power (See, for example, Bittner 1975; Colman and Gorman 1982; Dixon 1999; Freckleton and Selby 1989; Martin 1995; Newburn 2005; Reiner 1992). But the heart of the matter, explaining police power as such, remains under-theorised.

General treatments of policing, whether textbooks intended for those considering a policing career or scholarly works for an academic audience, noticeably dodge the issue. There will almost always be an early chapter which is a potted history of the "origins" of policing in the relevant jurisdictions. Hess et al. (2015), in the 11th edition of an American text, *Introduction to Law Enforcement and Criminal Justice*, is typical of the tribe. The Preface begins:

> Law enforcement and criminal justice in the United States have evolved tremendously since the country was founded over 200 years ago. Actually, the changes that have occurred in the past three decades alone are impressive. (Hess et al. 2015: xix)

Chapter 1 then "describes the evolution of law enforcement and the criminal justice system from its ancient roots to the present system" (Hess et al. 2015: xx). This narrative begins with the supposition "law enforcement can be traced back to cave dwellers", touches on some examples from ancient history, moves to English tithing and shire reeves, the birth of the New Police, then shifts focus to the United States and a more detailed administrative history of policing (Hess et al. 2015: 3–42).

A British example is Jason-Lloyd (2005). The first chapter is titled "The Development and Foundations of Modern Policing", and begins with the usual nod to pre-modern policing, then quotes from the *Metropolitan Police Act* 1829 which, it is said:

> signalled the formation of the first modern-style professional policing system in this country and, by 1856, all of England and Wales was covered by a network of police forces … Although in their early days the new police were often regarded with disdain and suspicion by both general populace and even some in authority, they quickly gained the respect still found amongst the majority of the public today. (Jason-Lloyd 2005: 3)

After seven paragraphs of history, the book moves to "The structure of policing in England and Wales", and matters of nomenclature and governing legislation.

A similar narrative arc, adjusted to suit the intended audience, is almost universal. Writers introduce the concept of the police, not by explaining what the police are but what they used to be. Against this background, a narrative of reform and modernisation unfolds. Later, such texts often attempt a summation of contemporary police-community relations. In Hess et al. (2015), the fourth chapter tackles the question "why we have police", but it is a cursory treatment. The authors assert that "Police authority comes from the people—their laws and institutions" (Hess et al. 2015: 121). In the American context, this refers specifically to the Constitution and the Bill of

Rights, along with "what the community wants … Because the success of policing depends heavily on public support, the citizens' wishes must be listened to and considered" (Hess et al. 2015: 121). The picture is vague, a suite of aphorisms which under scrutiny become tautologies. The one nod to theory is to briefly cite Egon Bittner's formulation that police are social agents who have the right and capacity to "address all sorts of human problems" in which "something-ought-not-to-be-happening-and-about-which-something-ought-to-be-done-NOW!" [original emphasis], using force if necessary (Hess et al. 2015: 120).

To an extent, the weakness of theory on police power is unsurprising, because power itself is notoriously slippery to define adequately (Stewart 2001). We address the theories of State power and how they might relate to policing below, but it is first necessary to touch on an area of scholarship which, at first glance appears promising, but which has a crucial weakness.

2.3 The Marxist Critique

What we call the Marxist critique is the view that police power can be understood as an aspect of the repressive capitalist State. By this view, police have an inherently politically "right" character. Writing in the 1970s, John Playford summarises the role of police in the Australian social order:

> Policemen… reinforce the conservative bias of government… Given their ideological orientation, they support with brutal zeal the determination of the civil power to combat left-wing ideas and movements… the police act as the coercive agents of the existing social order, particularly in periods of social strife or open class conflict. (Playford 1972: 139–140)

Seen in this light, the courts, the police and the armed forces are all means by which the capitalist State perpetuates itself (McQueen 1978). This is true even when class conflict is not obvious. The police adopt a "hegemonic" style, in which police are part of and work with the community to preserve order, but this "soft" approach to policing is underpinned by the capacity and willingness to use violent force (O'Malley 1983: ch. 4). Community policing, by this model, takes on a more sinister character: it is a means of social control which is cheaper, easier and more effective than direct and militaristic methods, but it is still primarily a way of preserving the capitalist order, a mode of social organisation which is exploitative and illegitimate.

In recent years there has been a revival of this analysis, often with the addition of aspects of Michel Foucault's ideas on the State and surveillance (Foucault 1979, 1982). To take one example of many, Neocleous (2014) argues:

> The police power … involves a set of apparatuses and technologies constituting political order in general and the law of labour in particular. This gives us an expanded concept of police that enables us to make sense of the fabrication of bourgeois order and is the very reason why that concept so central to police, namely security, is the fundamental concept of bourgeois society. (Neocleous 2014: 11)

Police power and war are the same thing:

> [T]he political lines of war continue into the subsequent peace, and peace itself is a coded war, then "keeping the peace" has to be understood anew, and it has to be understood anew through the concept which has historically been central to it as an idea: police. (Neocleous 2014: 9)

Further:

> war [is] inseparable from the history of capitalist domination. This book therefore seeks to understand the war power in terms of what is, after all, the most fundamental and violent conflict in human history: the class war. (Neocleous 2014: 6)

Such analyses of police and their function in society do make some valid points about the hypocrisy and double-talk which surrounds the police mission: to "keep the peace" through the threat of violence. However, there is a blind-spot at the heart of the argument. By ascribing policing and State violence to the capitalist social formation, it is implied that there must be an alternative: a society which can get by without police and without the threat of violence sanctioned by the State. Crime and, therefore, the need for police are the result of capitalism. A communist society, by supplying individual needs and eliminating inequality would, in Engels' words, "put an axe to the root of crime" (Bottomore 1991: 100).

In this book, we contend that the known human experience refutes this possibility. *All* societies protect their existing structures and power relations through violence and the threat of violence. This was true in pre-capitalist societies (see, for example, Egan 1996; Hämäläinen 2008) and is still true in traditional tribal societies (see, for example, Fagan 2018). It has been true of every revolutionary society, including those which have attempted to suppress and eliminate capitalism (to take just a few examples of literally thousands: Censer 2014; Ngor and Warner 1988; Kenez 2006; Slezkine 2017; Terrill 1999). There is not, to our knowledge, a single example of a sustained large-scale social system which has not been underpinned by violence and the threat of violence. That this is true of liberal capitalist societies, then, is wholly unsurprising.

2.4 Policing as a Social Function

Historians of policing frequently make the case that *policing* is a function of society, not of a particular organisation, and indeed that it predates *the police* as an institution (Johnston 1991). By this view the history of policing, in countries such as England, represents the gradual taking over by the State of what had previously been the rights and responsibilities of individuals or small groups (Rawlings 2002). For example, "bloodguilt", the right and duty of kin groups to avenge murder—laws described in detail in the Pentateuch, and still a feature of many traditional societies—was replaced by the crime of murder, the offenders being apprehended, prosecuted and punished by the agents of the State in the name of the community as a whole. This is the Hobbesian bargain: individuals surrender their rights to personal vengeance in return for the protection of the State (Hobbes 2005).

For a vivid illustration of the immense social benefits of this exchange, it is useful to look at the Icelandic sagas, which give a detailed picture of day-to-day life in the Icelandic Commonwealth. This was a pre-modern society with no central ruling authority. There were laws, which controlled in detail the lives of the people. However, the enforcement of those laws was up to individuals and their kin groups (Fidler and Gíslason 2017). The epic known as *Njal's Saga* (Magnusson and Hermann 1960) depicts a society in which the more responsible clan leaders use their influence and personal connections in an endless rear-guard action, seeking to prevent their community from destroying itself through worsening cycles of tit-for-tat violence. In medieval Icelandic society, policing was a shared responsibility given to the men of prominent families. As *Njal's Saga* illustrates, it was a dreadful model: it offered uncertain justice, caused needless loss of life and the destruction of property, and actually fostered violence and division.

In pre-modern societies, ruling elites faced great difficulties in meeting their part of the social contract. The power of most monarchs was theoretically near-absolute, but in practice their resources, not least for civil policing, were largely inadequate (Hughes 1994; Sperber 2017). The bureaucratic State, which emerged in nineteenth Century Europe, was typically constitutionally more limited than a traditional monarchy, but intruded into the lives of its subjects to a far greater extent. The creation of professional police "forces" was a signature feature of the shift from traditional to modern modes of administration. "Both obvious and ubiquitous," writes Steven Hughes, "the police symbolised a new personalised presence of the government in the people's everyday affairs" (Hughes 1994: 1).

The success of the Hobbesian social contract depends on the ruling elite being both competent and adequately resourced. If people are to surrender their personal rights to use force, then the promised protection from violence must be delivered. A professional police was a response to the crisis in civil order brought about by the growth of large industrial cities and improvements in transport. It was a crucial development for the ruling elites of the day, as the failure to ensure basic civil order creates a crisis of legitimacy, which in turn can be exploited by political rivals (Enders 2001). Contemporary "law and order" media campaigns, though usually cynical and exaggerated, are distant echoes of this real fear, that a weak or incompetent ruler would allow a breakdown in civil order (Martin 2019).

Such civic collapse is not just an historical fear. There are a great many communities in the modern world where ruling elites fail to deliver their end of the bargain: effective State policing. Modern Kenya, for example, has not succeeded in providing adequate public safety and services in vast areas of the capital city, Nairobi, where poor migrants from rural areas live in slum housing (Rasmussen 2010). In these areas, a gang-like mass organisation, the Mungiki emerged and established itself as de facto police (Rasmussen 2012). Similar instances where unofficial organisations provide security services, and where State police are either ineffective or non-existent, are documented all over the world, from Rio de Janeiro to Cape Town, from Hyderabad to Bali (Evans 2020).

Nor are such informal systems of policing confined to the developing world. In Northern Ireland, for example, some communities which are "hard-line" on one or other side of the political divide are effectively out of reach of the State police. Locally dominant paramilitary organisations provide a form of policing, a shadow justice system (Barbash 1995). Johnston notes that the operations of these "punishment squads", which give out beatings and other retribution for anti-social and criminal behaviour, are governed by widely understood rules. The actions of the squads are broadly accepted as legitimate within their communities, including by those who receive punishment (Johnston 1991: 163–164).

But while it is true that "policing" can be carried out in a range of ways, this book is predicated on the belief that a professional disciplined State police, overseen by democratic institutions and operating within known laws, has demonstrated its beneficence. With all its flaws acknowledged, it remains the best system for policing which has yet been devised.

2.5 Police as the Agents of Legitimate State Violence

Marxist theorists could save themselves a great deal of nuanced analysis by simply reading what the police, the guardians of liberal capitalist peace, say about their function. "I suppose I had better start by stating the obvious: that a degree of controlled violence is essential to government as we understand it." These are the words of Sir Robert Mark, then Commissioner of the London Metropolitan Police, writing in 1973. "Any form of government knows that it relies on the ultimate sanction of violence as the only certain means of preventing anarchy" (Mark 1973: 11). This is the modern State, as famously defined by Max Weber: "a human community that (successfully) claims the monopoly of the legitimate use of physical force within a given territory" (Weber 1948: 78). In a Weberian State, the function of policing is delegated to a professional, disciplined policing organisation, authorised to use violence within a set of rational laws.

It has long been usual for writers on policing to distinguish between the "civil police" of liberal democratic states, and "police states"—authoritarian regimes where the police are nakedly political (Chapman 1970; Tobias 1972). Common examples cited include Nazi Germany and the Soviet Union (Milte and Weber 1977: 8). This distinction is false. All societies, including the most authoritarian, need civil police to carry out the ordinary day-to-day functions of supervising and protecting the community: keeping peace between neighbours, regulating traffic, detecting and prosecuting non-political (which is to say, the vast majority of) offenders. Even in the most totalitarian of states, there are ordinary police doing these ordinary jobs: it was true in Nazi Germany and in the Soviet Union. The "political police," the Gestapo or NKVD, were more powerful and much feared, but the ordinary business of recovering stolen bicycles and keeping drunken young men out of trouble on Saturday nights was typically beneath their notice (Evans 2005; Plokhy 2018).

Societies vary in the extent to which they are inclusive, equitable and democratic, but in all conceivable social systems power is distributed unequally. Power is held by a ruling elite, however chosen. This is a matter of practical necessity: the exercise of power is a specialist function to which not all members of society are suited, or indeed aspire. By what has been called the "iron law of oligarchy", an elite, once established, tends to turn in on itself, becoming isolated and obsessed with internal struggles and self-perpetuation (Acemoglu and Robinson 2012; Diamond 2005).

Part of the reasoning behind the constitutional structures of the liberal democratic State is that by splitting powers and responsibilities between different arms of government, and allowing scrutiny of government through other institutions of civil society, the harm caused by the iron law of oligarchy is reduced. An independent and professional police is a vital part of this system. Police power underpins the power of parliaments, courts and the many bureaucracies essential to society. In David Bayley's memorable formulation: "Police are the leading edge of government regulation; what they do is part and parcel of government's activity; police and government could no more be separated than knife and knife-edge" (Bayley 1969: 11).

In his development of Bittner's theories on policing (Bittner 1975, 2005), Brodeur (2010) draws a distinction between military force, which will often be maximised to ensure annihilation of enemies, and police force, which must be limited to the minimum necessary. The reason for this limitation is that:

> … a great deal of police crisis intervention involves protecting all parties involved [including criminal offenders] … Since it would be self-defeating to use more force than is necessary to protect people from themselves, managing a crisis is not equivalent to clamping down on it. Using minimum force is not merely incidental to the police mandate, but constitutive of it. (Brodeur 2010: 108)

By this view, police are the sole agents of State violence "in comparison to softer internal controls, such as social work, which are superseded by police coercion in the context of developing crises. The police are who you call when all else is failing" (Brodeur 2010: 108). However, when a society is facing an existential threat and calls in military force, the force-use paradigm changes. Brodeur argues that the distinction between policing and military action is that policing is the "micromanagement of individual contingencies within the context of an established order *that remains unchallenged* … the police act on the presumption that breaches of certain parts of the established order do not signify that it is rejected as a whole" (Brodeur 2010: 109) [emphasis added]. That is, policing requires broad social consent—possibly grudging consent, but nonetheless misconduct occurs within the social system, and is not seeking its overthrow.

But what motivates community consent, perhaps reluctant, to the power of police? This consent appears to survive many shocks: even when police are exposed as corrupt or brutal, even when it is clear that police have used lethal force carelessly or criminally. In most communities the power of the police endures—perhaps damaged by scandal, but intact. That police power benefits police is obvious, but what of the policed community? What, so to speak, is in it for them? The answer is counter-intuitive: the policed community itself gains power.

2.6 The Monetary Model of Power

If, in Freidrich's famous phrase, "you cannot sit for long on bayonets" (Friedrich 1972: 3), what can you sit on? Sustained power must be based on authority, rather than force. That authority depends on a community of shared interests and values. To endure, any system of government—whether democratic and pluralist, or rigidly authoritarian—must convert coercive power to consensual power, through incentives, rewards and persuasion as well as force and intimidation (Friedrich 1972).

Paradoxically, one of the rewards for the surrender of power and freedom by individuals is an increase in the power and freedom available to those same individuals. Giving the role of policing to "the police", instead of keeping it within the community, gives power to the police *and* to the policed community. Power is often discussed as if it were a zero-sum exchange: if one sector of society gains in power, it must be at the expense of its rivals. In parliamentary elections, the zero-sum model applies, but such situations in which power is won or lost like ground in a rugby match are relatively rare. Power is not necessarily zero-sum; ideally the social contract allows individuals simultaneously to surrender and to gain power (Parsons 1963).

Braithwaite (1992) touches on this in what he calls the "republican" theory of policing. His argument is that police ideally provide citizens with the "freedom of the city", in which they are able to live their lives in the confident expectation of peace and security. Braithwaite contrasts this complex and subtle balance with the simple and libertarian "freedom of the heath", in which the weak are at the mercy of the strong. For most individuals, not only is the freedom of the city a more desirable state of affairs, it also increases the overall amount of power available to the wider community. Parsons (1963) proposes a "monetary" model of power. Just as a sound currency and banking system increases the overall money supply and can allow growth in the wealth of society as a whole, the institutions entrusted with power can further community interests. Real banks, by accepting deposits and advancing credit, allow people to use money which is not their own in productive ways; the "power banks" of the State similarly give people *the protection of power which is not their own*. A poor and physically weak person is protected from the abuse of others not just by his or her own power, but by the "borrowed" power of the police and the State. Trust is vital to the success of the system, as neither banks nor the agencies of power can fulfil all potential obligations if they are demanded in a short space of time.

Parsons conceives of power as a:

> generalized capacity to secure the performance of binding obligations by units in a system of collective organization when the obligations are legitimized with reference to their bearing on collective goals and where in case of recalcitrance there is a presumption of enforcement by negative situational sanctions—whatever the actual agency of that enforcement. (Parsons 1963: 237)

The most important such agency in modern society, the agency which will back up all the other agencies, using force if need be, is the police. In connection with police power the monetary model can be developed further. A money economy depends on an endless cycle of trust that pieces of paper and metal of no intrinsic value—not to mention digitised numbers on a computer—will be accepted as valuable by other people (Lanchester 2016). If something happens to destroy this trust, the value of currency can disappear with frightening speed. Similarly, police power depends on the widespread belief that it is far greater than is objectively the case. Police power is symbolically extended far beyond its physical reach.

Two well-known incidents, both from Australia, illustrate the strength of the illusion of police power, and the terrible consequences of its absence.

2.6.1 The Port Arthur Massacre

On Sunday 28 April 1996, Martin Bryant went on a killing spree at the Port Arthur historical site in Tasmania, killing 35 people and wounding scores more. The first police officer to arrive at the Broad Arrow Café, scene of the worst carnage, was Constable Brian Edmonds. Hundreds of people emerged from hiding when they saw him. Edmonds waited with them, alone, for twenty minutes before more police arrived. The situation was still confused. Edmonds could not be sure that the gunman—still at large and known to have several powerful weapons—would not reappear. Edmonds, who usually worked in search and rescue, was armed only with his service pistol, which had five rounds and was accurate to a range of 15 m (Flanagan 1997).

2.6.2 The Melbourne Police Strike

On the night of Thursday 31 October 1923, a group of uniformed constables in Melbourne, Victoria refused to parade for duty, demanding action on a range of workplace grievances. The following day, this wildcat industrial action spread, and about 600 police officers went on strike. As news of the strike spread, on Friday night, rioting and looting developed in the centre of Melbourne, and reached a violent climax the following evening. The last sporadic outbreaks of rioting were still being suppressed on Sunday afternoon. Three people were killed, many hundreds injured, and tens of thousands of pounds of damage was caused (Brown and Haldane 1998).

These two events underscore the paradox of police power. At Port Arthur, the near-instinctive faith so many people displayed, that one lightly-armed constable could protect them, was by any objective measure astonishingly naïve. But Brian Edmonds was far more than one police officer: he was "the police", the personal extension of *authority*, order, and the protection of the State from violence and disaster. Conversely, the mass outbreak of anti-social behaviour which occurred during the 1923 police strike cannot be explained by the diminution of the physical power of the police. There were 1808 sworn officers in Victoria Police in 1923. On the night of 1 November, about two-thirds of the force, some 1200 officers, did not strike. These police—hundreds more than would ordinarily have been on duty—were, in any case, rapidly augmented by the other resources of the State, including thousands of troops and special constables (Moore 1982). Almost all those charged with offences stemming from the riots during the Melbourne police strike were ordinary people who would normally be more-or-less law abiding (Brown and Haldane 1998). The notion that "the police were on strike" punctured the symbolic extension of police power, its illusory omnipotence, and resulted in violence and disaster.

To return to Parsons' monetary model of power, the Port Arthur incident can be likened to people placing their money with a trusted bank which is on the brink of insolvency, but which survives its liquidity crisis in part because it is so well trusted. The police strike can be compared to a financial panic, in which a rumour that a bank is insolvent causes a run on deposits and is very nearly self-fulfilling. The Melbourne police strike demonstrated starkly the frailty of police power. At full strength, before the strike, the ratio of police to the general population in Victoria was 1–902 (Brown and Haldane 1998: 30). This is a low figure historically, but were police numbers doubled, trebled, or even increased tenfold it would not change a simple truth. If the mass of people, for whatever reason, decide to go on a rampage the police will be completely overwhelmed.

2.7 Chapter Conclusion

Police power, like the value of money, is essentially symbolic. It depends on a shared illusion that it is much more robust than is objectively the case. It is precisely the symbolic nature of police power that makes the doctrine of minimum force, explored in Chap. 3, so important. Police are, on one hand, expected to intervene and solve all manner of tense, troublesome and difficult situations, and their capacity to use force is an essential part of being effective in this role. On the other hand, were police to actually use force in every instance where it might be justified, they would be exposed as not having the resources to do so, not to mention alienate many members of the policed community.

What Bittner describes as "the police's unique competence" (cited in Brodeur 2010: 116), the use of force, can only be successfully exercised if "police use of force is *potential rather than actual*. Its potential nature is what reconciles, in theory, the fact that it is all-encompassing with the requirement that it be minimal" [original emphasis] (Brodeur 2010: 116). Accepting that police power is socially beneficent, and accepting that this power is essentially symbolic, the question then arises. How should the power of police best be developed, maintained and projected? Critical to answering this question are considerations of how and when police use force, whether they should routinely carry firearms, and in what circumstances such weapons should be used. There are two broad streams of policing practice in this area: the doctrine of minimum force, explored in Chap. 3, and the more aggressive, armed tradition, examined in Chap. 4.

References

Acemoglu, D., & Robinson, J. A. (2012). *Why nations fail: The origins of power, prosperity and poverty*. New York: Crown Business.

Barbash, F. (1995). North Ireland's special terror; 'punishment' squads on both sides viciously discipline their own. *Washington Post*, 16 Feb, 1995.

Bayley, D. H. (1969). *Police and political development in India*. Princeton, NJ: Princeton University Press.

Bittner, E. (1975). *The functions of the police in modern society: A review of background factors, current practices, and possible role models*. New York: Jason Aronson.

Bittner, E. (2005). Florence Nightingale in pursuit of Willie Sutton: A theory of the police. In T. Newburn (Ed.), *Policing: Key readings*. Uffculme Cullompton: Willan.

Bottomore, T. B. (1991). *A dictionary of Marxist thought*. Oxford: Blackwell.

Braithwaite, J. (1992). Good and bad police services and how to pick them. In P. Moir & H. Eijkman (Eds.), *Policing Australia: Old issues, new perspectives*. Melbourne: Macmillan.

Brodeur, J.-P. (2010). *The policing web*. Oxford: Oxford University Press.

Brown, G., & Haldane, R. (1998). *Days of violence: The 1923 police strike in Melbourne*. Melbourne: Hybrid.

Censer, J. R. (2014). Historians revisit the terror—Again. *Journal of Social History, 48,* 383–403.

Chapman, B. (1970). *Police state*. London: Pall Mall Press.

Chatterton, M. (1973). Sociology and the police. In J. C. Alderson & P. J. Stead (Eds.), *The police we deserve*. London: Wolfe.

Clarke, R. (1972). Police that serve society. In R. M. Hutchins & M. J. Adler (Eds.), *The great ideas today*. Chicago: Encyclopedia Britannica.

Colman, M., & Gorman, L. P. (1982). Conservatism, dogmatism and authoritarianism in British police officers. *Sociology, 16,* 1–11.

Diamond, J. (2005). *Collapse: How societies choose to fail or survive*. London: Allen Lane.

Dixon, D. (1999). The normative structure of policing. In D. Dixon (Ed.), *A culture of corruption: Changing an Australian police service* (pp. 69–97). Sydney: Hawkins Press.

Dubber, M. D. (2005). *The police power: Patriarchy and the foundations of American government*. New York: Columbia University Press.

Egan, T. (1996). *Justice all their own: The Caledon Bay and Woodah Island killings 1932–1933*. Melbourne: Melbourne University Press.

Enders, M. (2001). The social construction of crime and policing. In M. Enders & B. Dupont (Eds.), *Policing the lucky country*. Sydney: Federation Press.

Evans, R. J. (2005). *The Third Reich in power, 1933–1939*. London: Allen Lane.

Evans, R. (2020). 'A combination of extortion and civic duty': A comparative criminological perspective on informal security organisations in Bali. In A. Vandenberg (Ed.), *Community security, democracy and society in Bali*. Palgrave.

Fagan, C. (2018). Shuri carries a wooden bow and two six-foot arrows topped with razor-sharp bamboo. *National Geographic, 234*(4), 66.

Fidler, R., & Gíslason, K. (2017). *Saga land*. Sydney: HarperCollins.

Flanagan, M. (1997). Lest we forget. *The Age*, Saturday Extra, April 12.

Foucault, M. (1979). *Discipline and punish: The birth of the prison*. New York: Vintage.

Foucault, M. (1982). The subject and power. *Critical Inquiry, 8*(Summer), 777–795.

Freckleton, I., & Selby, H. (1989). Piercing the blue veil: An assessment of external review of police. In D. Chappell & P. Wilson (Eds.), *Australian policing: Contemporary issues*. Sydney: Butterworths.

Friedrich, C. J. (1972). Opposition and government by violence. *Government and Opposition, 7*(1), 3–19.

Golding, W. (1960). *Lord of the flies*. Harmondsworth: Penguin.

Hämäläinen, P. (2008). *The Comanche empire.* New Haven: Yale University Press.

Hess, K. M., Orthmann, C. M. H., & Cho, H. L. (2015). *Introduction to law enforcement and criminal justice.* New York: Thomas.

Hobbes, T. (2005). *Of man.* London: Penguin.

Hughes, S. (1994). *Crime, disorder and the risorgimento: The politics of policing in Bologna.* Cambridge: Cambridge University Press.

Jason-Lloyd, L. (2005). *Introduction to policing and police powers.* London: Routledge-Cavendish.

Johnston, L. (1991). *The rebirth of private policing.* London: Routledge.

Kenez, P. (2006). *A history of the Soviet Union from the beginning to the end.* Cambridge: Cambridge University Press.

Lanchester, J. (2016). When bitcoin grows up. *London Review of Books, 38*(8), 3–12.

Macleod, R. C., & Schneiderman, D. (1994). *Police powers in Canada: The evolution and practice of authority.* Toronto: University of Toronto Press.

Magnusson, M., & Hermann, P. (1960). *Njal's saga.* Harmondsworth: Penguin.

Mark, R. (1973). Social violence. In J. C. Alderson & P. J. Stead (Eds.), *The police we deserve.* London: Wolfe.

Martin, M. A. (1995). *Urban policing in Canada: Anatomy of an aging craft.* Montreal: McGill-Queen's University Press.

Martin, G. (2019). *Crime, media and culture.* Milton: Taylor & Francis Group.

McQueen, H. (1978). Shoot the Bolshevik! Hang the profiteer! Reconstructing Australian capitalism. In E. L. Wheelwright & K. Buckley (Eds.), *Essays in the political economy of Australian capitalism.* Sydney: Australia and New Zealand Book Co.

Milte, K., & Weber, T. (1977). *Police in Australia: Development, functions, procedures.* Sydney: Butterworths.

Moore, A. (1982). Guns across the Yarra: Secret armies and the 1923 Melbourne police strike. In Sydney Labour History Group (Ed.), *What rough beast?: The state and social order in Australian history.* Sydney: Allen & Unwin.

Neocleous, M. (2014). *War power, police power.* Edinburgh: Edinburgh University Press.

Newburn, T. (2005). *Policing: Key readings.* Uffculme Collumpton: Willan.

Ngor, H., & Warner, R. (1988). *Surviving the killing fields: The Cambodian odyssey of Haing S. Ngor.* London: Chatto & Windus.

O'Malley, P. (1983). *Law, capitalism and democracy.* Sydney: Allen & Unwin.

Parsons, T. (1963). On the concept of political power. *Proceedings of the American Philosophical Society, 107*(3), 232.

Playford, J. (1972). Who rules Australia. In J. Playford & D. Kirsner (Eds.), *Australian capitalism: Towards a Marxist critique.* Melbourne: Penguin.

Plokhy, S. (2018). *Chernobyl: History of a tragedy.* London: Allen Lane.

Rasmussen, J. (2010). Mungiki as youth movement: Revolution, gender and generational politics in Nairobi, Kenya. *YOUNG, 18*(3), 301–319.

Rasmussen, J. (2012). Inside the system, outside the law: Operating the Matatu sector in Nairobi. *Urban Forum, 23,* 415–432.

Rawlings, P. (2002). *Policing: A short history.* Uffculme Cullompton: Willan.

Reiner, R. (1992). *The politics of the police.* Hemel Hempstead: Harvester Wheatsheaf.

Slezkine, Y. (2017). *The house of government: A saga of the Russian Revolution.* Princeton, NJ: Princeton University Press.

Sperber, J. (2017). *Revolutionary Europe, 1780–1850.* Abingdon, Oxford: Routledge.

Stewart, A. M. A. (2001). *Theories of power and domination: The politics of empowerment in late modernity.* London: Sage.

Stobbs, N. (2009). Police power and duties. In R. G. Broadhurst & S. Davies (Eds.), *Policing in context: An introduction to police work in Australia.* Melbourne: Oxford University Press.

Terrill, R. (1999). *Mao: A biography.* Stanford: Stanford University Press.

Tobias, J. J. (1972). Police and public in the United Kingdom. *Journal of Contemporary History, 7*(1/2), 201–219.
Weber, M. (1948). Politics as a vocation. In H. H. Gerth & C. W. Mills (Eds.), *Max Weber: Essays in sociology*. London: Routledge & Kegan Paul.

Chapter 3
'Only the Minimum Degree': The Minimum Force Tradition

Abstract The doctrine of minimum force is deeply engrained across policing scholarship and practice. To understand its origin, writers typically look to the 1829 creation of the New Police in London, and "Peel's Principles". Despite an uncertain provenance, the Principles remain enormously influential. In this chapter, we explore the surprisingly flimsy theoretical underpinning of minimum force policing. Among the more substantial contributions in this field are Egon Bittner's theories on policing and the use of force, and David Bayley's examination of police organisations as political actors in their own right. However, we argue that there remains a lack of a coherent theory underpinning the minimum force doctrine, and that this is of concern. In many jurisdictions police are becoming increasingly militarized, and there is growing pressure for officers to take a more aggressive approach in their dealings with offenders, as discussed in Chap. 4.

3.1 Introduction

The doctrine of minimum force is deeply engrained in understandings and discussions of policing. Almost every text on policing will contain a passage similar to these:

> The key principle underlying the use of force is that the force used be the minimum necessary to achieve legitimate objectives and should be proportionate and reasonable in the circumstances. In policing terms, this stems from a combination of "policing by consent" and the standard of "minimum force" (Palmer 2017: 386).

> The use of force by police officers is subject to control … police powers frequently include such formulae as "using no more force than reasonably necessary" … the general test of "reasonable force" is that it was justified in the circumstances at the time (Edwards 1999: 171).

> Police officers should be trained in the doctrine of minimum force by replacing the word "reasonable" with words such as "minimal", "absolutely necessary" and "proportionate" … This gives primacy to low-level uses of force, and the proportionate response rules out any high-level force once a citizen has already been subdued (Buttle 2010: 35).

These are uncontroversial statements to which no scholar of policing is likely to object. The expectation of minimum force is also enshrined in documents such as

R. Evans and C. Farmer, *Do Police Need Guns?*,
https://doi.org/10.1007/978-981-15-9526-4_3

21

the United Nations' Code of Conduct for Law Enforcement Officials: "Law enforcement officials may use force only when strictly necessary and to the extent required for the performance of their duty" (United Nations 1979: Article 3). Similarly, the *United Kingdom Human Rights Act* 1998, by virtue of Article 2(2) of the European Convention on Human Rights, while acknowledging that the State may use force against a person, up to and including lethal force, specifies: "the force used must be essential and strictly proportionate. Force is 'proportionate' when it is appropriate and no more than necessary to address the problem concerned" (Equality and Human Rights Commission 2019). It is surprising, then, that drilling down to establish from where the minimum force doctrine originates, and what theories underpin it, is a difficult task.

In this chapter we interrogate the doctrine of minimum-force policing. We first draw attention to the uncertain and fluid framework upon and within which minimum force has been operationalised, and the lack of consensus about both policy and practice, exemplified by debates regarding policing by consent, de-escalation, excessive force, police discretion and legitimacy. The relationship between the embedded doctrine of minimum force policing and the normalisation of routinely armed police is then examined—emphasising the disconnect between the concept and operation of minimum force. In conclusion, we argue for robust and ongoing empirical research to test the efficacy of the doctrine of minimum force and, in particular, to examine the effects of routinely armed policing.

3.2 Minimum Force and 'Peel's Principles'

In his celebratory short history of the British police, published in 1948, Charles Reith waxes lyrical about how, despite deeply entrenched hostility, Sir Robert Peel's New Police won over public opinion:

> They [police officers] were told that they must cultivate good relations with the public by combining modesty and firmness. And dignity of manner and address, with good humour and kindly friendliness, and by showing infinite patience under provocation. They were taught to behave in a manner that would induce the public to regard them as friends and servants, and to see the exercise of their authority as policemen was neither bullying nor tyrannical, but simply and solemnly a service to the public. By quiet and unobtrusive fulfilment of these instructions, the police eventually conquered public hostility ... (Reith 1948: 63).

Notable is the use of the passive voice. "They *were told* ... They *were taught* ... fulfilment of *these instructions.*" From where did this advice originate? Reith admired Charles Rowan and Richard Mayne, the joint commissioners of London's Metropolitan Police at its founding in 1829, and gives them much of the credit for the new style adopted and for its success. Rowan and Mayne, Reith argues, had an early vision of "the close and friendly relationship between the police and the public" which eventuated. Reith describes this development as a "miracle," especially given initial public hostility (Reith 1948: 44).

Towards the end of his book, without much explanation, Reith lists "nine police principles" (1948: 94). To focus on what is most relevant to the present discussion: police are instructed (Principle 6) "to use physical force only when the exercise of persuasion, advice and warning is found to be insufficient … and to use only the minimum degree of physical force which is necessary on any particular occasion". Why? Because (Principle 2) "the power of the police to fulfil their functions and duties is dependent on public approval of their existence, actions and behaviour and on their ability to secure and maintain public respect". Absent such respect (Principle 1) "crime and disorder" would require "their repression by military force and severity of legal punishment".

Some odd features are evident with respect to these injunctions, which are often referred to as "Peel's Principles," after Sir Robert Peel. There are at least four different versions of the Principles in circulation: two with twelve principles, one with ten, and one (that originating with Reith) with nine (Lentz and Chaires 2007). While there is much overlap, only the nine-principle list specifically enjoins minimum force and so is the focus here. In their detailed study of the origins of the various published versions of the Principles, Lentz and Chaires (2007) note how in policing textbooks the Principles are usually simply reproduced and expected, as it were, to speak for themselves: "What a student is supposed to make of such 'principles' remains problematic. This is unfortunate, because all the various versions require analysis and explanation" (Lentz and Chaires 2007: 73).

As Lentz and Chaires demonstrate, there is no evidence that Sir Robert Peel had anything to do with the drafting of the Principles. They do not appear as part of the legislation which created the New Police, nor in the General Instructions which were issued to every new police officer in 1829. Rather, Peel's Principles "are an invention of twentieth century policing textbooks" (Lentz and Chaires 2007: 69). The earliest known version of the Principles which appears in list form is the one in Reith's 1948 book. Reith had access to original documents held in the Scotland Yard library, but he does not cite his sources. Nor does he claim the principles are associated with Peel, or derived from an historic document. Rather, the list appears in a chapter titled "British Police Today", and is presented as an evolved set of dicta which helps the reader understand what Reith views as contemporary best practice (Reith 1948: 94).

As Lentz and Chaires note: "[t]hat Peel's principles were invented, however, does not necessarily make them a fiction" (2007: 70). Regardless of origins, they have been and remain enormously influential. The UK Home Office still has them displayed on its website, where they are intended to provide a "definition of policing by consent" (Home Office (UK) 2012). Similarly, in a document outlining strategy for policing to 2025, Australia's Victoria Police declares: "The principles established by Sir Robert Peel in 1829 when he created the London Metropolitan Police, remain relevant today and inform many aspects of the Vision [for Victoria Police]," and reproduces a slightly modified nine-point list (Victoria Police 2014: 9).

Any attempt to find sources for the doctrine of minimum force policing seems to loop back to Charles Reith, and the Policing Principles he published in 1948, the origins of which remain obscure. At some point, one or more people involved in British policing wrote down the doctrine of minimum force. This event may have occurred in the days of Charles Rowan and Richard Mayne, or it may not. The principles articulate an approach to the use of force which has been hugely influential, but what underpins the doctrine of minimum-force policing? Despite almost two centuries of the practice, the theory remains thin.

3.3   Accident or Inevitable?

Reith presents the idea of policing by consent, and the embedded doctrine of minimum force, as a lucky accident (Reith 1948, 1952). Rowan and Mayne, the two men who created the first modern police service, appeared to have a hunch that minimum force was the best approach, and it happened to work. Reith argues that previous conventional thinking had been that police must be "wholly repressive" (Reith 1948: 61) in order to be effective. What he calls the "discovery" (p. 94) that this was not the case unlocked the path to "miracles in the science and art of policing" (p. 63). The New Police proved a success in London, and the model of an unarmed civilian police who were themselves subject to the law was rapidly taken up in other, though not all, parts of Britain and the British Empire (Critchley 1977). But was this a unique event, depending on the insights and personalities of two reforming public servants? Or would the pressing social problems created by urbanisation and industrialisation have led inexorably to the creation of something similar to the New Police?

Perhaps the most considered examination of the evolution of the use of force by police is found in the work of Egon Bittner (Bittner 1975). He argues that the emergence of modern policing is part of a gradual reduction of personal violence in society, a broad social movement both facilitated by and necessary to a modern world of advanced economies and large cities in which strangers must peacefully coexist. The use of force has been removed from almost every aspect of life in modern society: "paper, not the sword, is the instrument of coercion of our day" (Bittner 2005: 166). The gradual move towards a less-violent society has little to do with high motives, such as political conviction or religious faith. Rather, driving the change is "the lacklustre ethic of utilitarianism" (Bittner 1975: 20). The common good (greater peace) coincides with the personal good:

> Our desire to abolish violence is fundamentally based not on the belief that it is spiritually reprehensible, but on the realisation that it is foolish. Forceful attack and the defence it provokes have an unfavourable input/output ratio; they are a waste of energy. A simple, hardheaded, business-like calculus dictates that coercive force, especially of a physical nature, is at best an occasionally unavoidable evil (Bittner 1975: 20).

But no matter how thoroughly force is removed from the routine business of life, in the end the capacity to use force must exist: "… the only practical way of banishing the use of force from life generally is to assign its residual exercise—where according to circumstances it appears unavoidable—to a specially deputised corps of officials, that is, to the police as we know it" (Bittner 2005: 166). Bittner argues that the potential for the use of force is the defining characteristic of modern policing. There is an astonishing variety of situations to which police might be called, but there is a common thread:

> The policeman, and the policeman alone, is equipped, entitled, and required to deal with every exigency in which force may have to used, to meet it. Moreover, the authorization to use force is conferred upon the policeman with the mere proviso that force will be used in amounts measured not to exceed the necessary minimum, as determined by an intuitive grasp of the situation (Bittner 2005: 165).

By this view, the minimum force doctrine is merely pragmatic. To be effective, the police need public support, and that is endangered if police use force which is perceived to be "excessive". However, that assessment—what is excessive force in any given situation—is a cultural, situational and individual construct. It can and does vary, and so can be the object of political struggle. Minimum force may, it is true, be the product of "the lacklustre ethic of utilitarianism," but political actors need to perceive that utility, and articulate and push for it. That, Reith argues, was the achievement of Rowan and Mayne (Reith 1948, 1952). By listing his "Principles of Policing," and by hoping to demonstrate what he regarded as the singular genius of "British Police Today," Reith was attempting to do the same thing.

The contest over which philosophy should underpin policing is long-running. In his seminal 1969 study of policing, David Bayley notes the poles of opinion.

> Does the readiness of police to use force call forth hostility and violence in the general public, and particularly among suspects, or is readiness to use force essential to prevent a greater amount of violence from the public and suspects? It is illuminating to note that police authorities in the United States and Great Britain proceed on the basis of diametrically opposed theories in this matter, for the British policeman does not carry a firearm, the American policeman always does. Police authorities in Britain believe that to go armed, to prepare visibly for war, would trigger a greater amount of violence among those they contact; American police, on the other hand, believe that their sidearm is an essential deterrent, and without it they would be helpless in enforcing the law (Bayley 1969: 24).

At the time Bayley was writing, there was little evidence to support either position. Both were matters of faith and custom. Writing decades later, Bayley (2002) further explores whether there is a tension between observing due process, such as respect for human rights, and police effectiveness. He concludes that there is not:

> … the choice between hard (deterrent) and soft (rule-of-law) policing is false. In order to become effective at preventing crime, police need to be protective of human rights so that they can enlist the willing cooperation of the public. Policing by consent, to use the British slogan, is more effective at crime prevention and control than is hard-nosed law enforcement by socially isolated police (Bayley 2002: 142–143).

By contrast with his 1969 writings, here Bayley (2002) is able to draw on a great deal of published research which supports the importance to police effectiveness of public support and cooperation. This includes Bayley's own discussions of policing by consent (1985) and democratic policing (1999), and Skolnick and Fyfe's (1993) investigation of policing and excessive force. The process has continued. More recent comparative studies emphasise the great variations which exist internationally with respect to police use of force, in terms of formal legal rules and normative community standards (Knutsson and Kuhns 2010). Interwoven with the acknowledgment of variations in expectations of police is the complex area of police discretion (Bronitt and Stenning 2011). It is noteworthy that in their discussion of police discretion, Bronitt and Stenning acknowledge the topic's semi-mythological origins with the New Police and "Peel's Principles" which "do not address the issue of discretion directly, but the idea of discretion underscores several of them" (Bronitt and Stenning 2011: 323).

Others have explored this issue under the rubric of "legitimacy," arguing that a broad public perception of legitimacy is a pre-requisite for effective policing (Tyler 2006; Tyler and Wakslak 2004). Legitimacy can be engendered by and manifested through a range of contexts, such as police effectiveness and procedural justice, as viewed by the policed community (Bradford and Jackson 2016; Huq et al. 2017; Tyler and Jackson 2014). A key element in the perceived legitimacy of police is community acceptance that officers use force appropriately and in accordance with public expectations: both are embodied within the doctrine of minimum force.

However, the argument can become circular. There are aphoristic statements, such as "[w]hen police act beyond the law, they lose their moral authority" (Bayley 2002: 143). Such contentions are supported by research studies of public attitudes, but it is acknowledged that attitudes can differ depending on the place and time (Bayley 1995). This context, in turn, does not occur in a vacuum. To cite one example of many, in their study of media discourse surrounding police use of lethal force in the United States, Hirschfield and Simon (2010) demonstrate that police violence is usually framed in such a way that police actions are justified and legitimised, while victims are often demonised. Police legitimacy requires that officers meet public expectations about the use of force, but public expectations are influenced by many factors, including media coverage, views expressed by authority figures, and the words and actions of the police themselves.

One of Bayley's key insights is that a society's police are not just reflective of that society and its institutions; rather, police are important political actors (Bayley 1969: 152). How police act, and especially how they choose to use their special privileges in relation to violence, has a significant role in shaping the policed community (Heslop 2015). To test this contention, it is necessary to look again at the story of the New Police.

3.4 Does Minimum Force Require Peace, or Create It?

As a model of policing, minimum force—which was what the British New Police did in practice, whether or not it was a matter of instruction—represented a significant break with convention. The important fact about the New Police was that they were unarmed, and were not overtly ruthless or oppressive in their behaviour towards the policed community (Palmer 1988). As an approach to policing, perhaps to the surprise of many, it worked. Reith claims that the New Police:

eliminated the need of repression of disorder by military force and the infliction of civilian casualties. They created liberty and personal security for individuals which initiated an immense expansion of social intercourse and amenities. They eliminated the need of carrying arms (Reith 1952: 171).

The reality cannot have been so clear-cut, nor so rapid. Later police historians have problematized the "march of progress" narrative, questioning both the reputed ineptitude of traditional policing prior to 1829, and the rapid success of the New Police afterwards (Devereaux 2001). Taylor's (1997) scrupulous study of early English policing agrees that progress towards public acceptance of the New Police was slow and uneven, but concludes that by the end of the nineteenth century, the English police officer was indeed a broadly accepted figure among the community. Ackroyd's (2000) history of London surveys both the competing historical views and the evidence of contemporary sources on the issue and concludes: "against the records of the violence and energy of the London crowd [prior to 1829], we must place this evidence of almost instinctive obedience" to police (Ackroyd 2000: 289). This attitude cannot have been universal:

> The statistics of attacks upon the police, then and now, are testimony to that. But the observers are correct in one general respect. There does seem to be a critical point or mass at which the city somehow calms itself down and does not consume itself in general riot or insurrection. A level of instability is reached, only to retreat (Ackroyd 2000: 289).

Of course, the "close and friendly relationship between the police and the public" which Reith could boast of in 1948 (44) was exposed to many strains and shocks in subsequent decades. Writing in the early 1970s, Reith's fellow police historian T.A. Critchley expresses the worry that the social changes of his day—increased individualism, the breakdown of traditional communities, and the like—place the tradition of minimum force and policing by consent under threat (Critchley 1973). He argues that only stable and homogenous societies with broadly accepted laws can hope to develop policing by consent in this way, and attributes the success of the English police model in the nineteenth and early twentieth centuries to just such a broad social consensus. This argument seems obviously false. The New Police were started in large part *because of* serious and worsening social divisions, and they were not warmly or immediately welcomed (Storch 1975). Support for the police was at first both sectoral and fragile, and police officers had a difficult task in negotiating their role in urban neighbourhoods (Ignatieff 1979).

Reith (1948) highlights the violence and rejection the New Police faced, and argues that it was precisely the unarmed, minimum-force character of the new organisation which allowed it to succeed and, over time, to act in its own right as a stabilising factor in the community. Reith reports American visitors to Britain in the 1940s expressing the view that the British policing style was "soft", and was only possible because the British people were even softer, indeed "sheep".

> If he had the opportunity of seeing a baton charge, or the police in action … [when it was needed] to make use of their own force … he would have found reason to change his mind. The degree of physical force which is sometimes the minimum that is necessary for the achievement of a police objective can be extremely formidable (Reith 1948: 111).

That such force rarely needed to be used was, Reith argues, *a consequence of* the minimum force doctrine. Reith's writings on the excellence of British policing seem complacent to the modern reader, but still he has a point. This is illustrated by another historical example of the creation of an unarmed police service. Though less well known—it is absent from any policing textbook the present authors have found— the An Garda Siochana in the Republic of Ireland is perhaps a more compelling operationalisation of the minimum force doctrine than even that of the New Police.

Prior to 1922, Ireland was policed by the Royal Irish Constabulary (RIC), which was armed, centralised and operated from barracks. As the struggle for Irish independence intensified in the early twentieth century, the RIC came to be seen as an agent of oppression, a tool of the British hegemony (Brewer et al. 1996: 86). In 1922, Ireland won partial independence through armed struggle. The Anglo-Irish Treaty created the Irish Free State (later the Republic of Ireland) but at the expense of accepting partition and the creation of Northern Ireland. Hard-line Republicans denied the legitimacy of the Free State and took up arms against its government, leading to civil war. In the midst of this chaos, the new Irish state had to establish a police service (Brady 1974). As is common in the post-colonial experience, existing institutions were adopted. The police was given a new name, An Garda Siochana ("guardians of the peace"), but most of its officers were veterans of the RIC, and existing structures and ranks were maintained (Mulroe 2016). It was, however, transformed into an unarmed force. McNiffe (1997: 26) argues: "Disarming the emerging force was perhaps the most significant contribution to ensuring it became a civilian rather than a semi-military body". McNiffe makes the case that it was precisely the unarmed character of the new force which was the key to its success.

> The decision … to send out unarmed policemen was both courageous and ambitious. In many respects the new force had modelled itself very closely on its predecessor, the RIC, but this was a clear break with tradition. This decision influenced the public perception of the force and greatly facilitated its acceptance by all sides of the community. It was, perhaps, the most significant decision taken by any government concerning the Garda … (McNiffe 1997: 96).

Like many police services, the Garda has faced major scandals over corruption and malpractice in recent decades (Manning 2012; O'Sullivan 2015). What is notable, though, is that the question of arming the Garda is nowhere raised as part of a reform program. Arming is not rejected; it is not even raised as a possibility.

The Irish example lends support to Reith's thesis that the very fact of a police service being unarmed is a de-escalating factor in terms of levels of violence in society more generally, and against police in particular. However, this suggestion runs counter to contemporary trends. In almost every jurisdiction, police are becoming increasingly militarised in their uniforms and equipment, to be armed if they are not already so, or to carry more and more powerful weapons if they are (Farmer and Evans 2019).

3.5 Chapter Conclusion

An unarmed police service, whose members do not have lethal force immediately and invariably available, is the bodily incarnation of the minimum force doctrine. It is making manifest the confidence that the police are accepted by the community, that the need for force will be rare, and the need for lethal force rarer still. However, there is increasing pressure on this position. In both New Zealand and Great Britain, two jurisdictions where police have eschewed the routine carriage of firearms, there has been considerable recent pressure for police to be armed.

In 2010, following a survey of NZ Police Association (NZPA) members, 72% supported the routine arming of officers and the NZPA promoted this change as a way to increase the safety of police officers (Police News 2010). Opinion fluctuated in the years that followed, but intensified again following the terror attack in Christchurch in 2019. At the time of writing, New Zealand Police are trialling the use of "Armed Response Teams," intended to support regular operational police who will continue to not carry firearms (Guardian 2019). This decision has been met with protest and unease among some New Zealanders, and the Police Commissioner has conceded that opinion within the police service is divided on the issue (Bhatia 2019; Bond 2019a, b). In Great Britain, a number of high-profile incidents and perceived changes in criminal behaviour, such as a rise in random knife crime, have caused the routine arming of police to be questioned more openly (Eustachewich 2018). Late in 2018, London's Metropolitan Police confirmed the deployment of routinely armed patrols in a number of high crime areas, with officers carrying their firearms visibly (Dodd 2018).

Two points need to be made about the pressure to arm police.

First, while it can be argued that the minimum force doctrine of policing is compatible with routinely arming police—and many routinely-armed jurisdictions have formal minimum force doctrines—the very fact of police carrying firearms represents a shift in tone and approach from that of the unarmed "New Police".

Second, this chapter has probed the doctrine of minimum force policing and found it to be thinly supported. However, it is necessary to stress that the same is true of the opposing philosophy, what we have termed the "armed tradition" of policing. Striking by its absence is a theoretical or evidentiary basis for the expectation that police and the community are safer when police routinely carry firearms than when they do not. As is examined in Chapter 4, that carrying firearms increases safety is simply asserted, presented as an unchallenged and unchallengeable truth. There has been some questioning of the nature and form of police firearms *training*, and its utility to police in practice (Morrison and Vila 1998). However, there is little evidence to support the basic effectiveness of a firearm in improving officer or community safety.

The evolution of police firearms policy in the United Kingdom has been largely reactive: incidents in which unarmed police have failed to prevent a tragedy lead to pressure for increased police access to and deployment of firearms; incidents in which armed police kill or seriously wound a non-offender increase concern about armed police, and the need for non-lethal alternatives to firearms (Rogers 2003).

Waldren (2007) presents part of the reason for arming police as a matter of morale: in the wake of violence, especially lethal violence directed at police, officers feel exposed and unsafe without weapons of their own. However, he notes the essentially symbolic nature of the routine arming of police:

> the chances of an armed confrontation when on routine foot patrol, are remote. The reality is that the officers are there to be seen–a clear signal that the police are taking a particular problem seriously, that they have guns and that they are prepared to use them (Waldren 2007: 261).

Hendy (2014), drawing on Squires and Kennison (2010), also refers to morale, but adds a complicating factor. Officers who are armed "feel safer," but this is not necessarily justified. Indeed, the greater confidence resulting from the possession of a firearm may make officers more likely to expose themselves to dangerous situations, and actually increase their risk of injury (Hendy 2014).

Discussing the more militarised appearance adopted by a (not routinely-armed) police service in Great Britain, De Camargo (2016) demonstrates that there is self-awareness among police of the implications of the "military look". She quotes an officer:

> At least part of the rationale for a military trickle-down is emotional. When we wear these details, we are wearing safety; we wrap ourselves in a little bit of military security and feel more protected somehow (De Camargo 2016: 120).

Hendy (2014) reveals similar feelings of protection and safety in his study of Norwegian (unarmed) and Swedish (armed) police. One Swedish officer is quoted saying: "I would feel naked to go out [on patrol] without a gun. I could not do it now because I started with a gun …" (Hendy 2014: 188).

While the work of researchers such as Hendy are beginning to fill the gaps in our understanding of policing and weapons, the debate over arming police remains largely rhetorical and symbolic. In the blue corner, as it were, are Peel's Principles and Charles Reith: "The success of the British police lies in the fact that they represent the discovery of a process for transmuting crude, physical force" (Reith 1952: 162). In the red corner is police armament presented as a matter of "common sense". Scott Weber, chief executive of the Police Federation of Australia, which represents Australian (routinely armed) police, told an audience of New Zealand (not routinely armed) police:

> It boggles our minds that you guys don't wear guns on your hips. What is it doing in the boot of your car when you are dealing with a violent offender? You need every tactical option ready to rock'n'roll (Police News 2019).

Weber's statement encapsulates what we term the "armed tradition" of policing. This is the uncritical assumption that police always need immediate access to lethal weapons, both to be effective in protecting the community, and for their own safety. In the next chapter, we unpack and interrogate the armed tradition of policing. We argue that this "common sense" position has neither a coherent theoretical base nor real-world evidence to support its contentions.

References

Ackroyd, P. (2000). *London: The biography*. London: Chatto & Windus.

Bayley, D. H. (1969). *Police and political development in India*. Princeton, N.J.: Princeton University Press.

Bayley, D. H. (1995). Police brutality abroad. In W. Geller & H. Toch (Eds.), *And justice for all: Understanding and controlling police abuse of force*. Washington, D.C.: Police Executive Research Forum.

Bayley, D. H. (2002). Law enforcement and the rule of law: Is there a tradeoff? *Criminology and Public Policy, 2*(1), 133–154.

Bhatia, R. (2019). *Strong opposition to planned armed police units*. Stuff.co.nz, 2 Nov.

Bittner, E. (1975). *The functions of the police in modern society: A review of background factors, current practices, and possible role models*. New York: Jason Aronson.

Bittner, E. (2005). Florence Nightingale in pursuit of Willie Sutton: A theory of the police. In T. Newburn (Ed.), *Policing: Key Readings*. Uffculme Cullompton: Willan.

Bond, J. (2019a). Auckland residents protest as number of armed police officers grows. *New Zealand Herald*, 3 Nov.

Bond, J. (2019b). Police armed response team arrest in suburban area raises concerns. *New Zealand Herald*, 11 Nov.

Bradford, B., & Jackson, J. (2016). Enabling and constraining police power: On the moral regulation of policing. In J. Jacobs & J. Jackson (Eds.), *Routledge Handbook of Criminal Justice Ethics*. Oxon: Routledge.

Brady, C. (1974). *Guardians of the peace*. Dublin: Gill and Macmillan.

Brewer, J. D., Guelke, A., Hume, I., et al. (1996). *The police, public order and the state: Policing in Great Britain, Northern Ireland, the Irish Republic, the USA, Israel, South Africa and China*. Basingstoke, UK: Macmillan.

Bronitt, S., & Stenning, P. (2011). Understanding discretion in modern policing. *Criminal Law Journal, 35*(6), 319–332.

Buttle, J. (2010). Officer safety and public safety: Training the police to use force in the United Kingdom. In J. Knutsson, J. B. Kuhns (Eds.), *Police Use of Force: A Global Perspective*. Santa Barbara, Calif.: Praeger.

Critchley, T. A. (1973). The idea of policing in Britain: Success or failure. In J. C. Alderson & P. J. Stead (Eds.), *The police we deserve*. London: Wolfe.

Critchley, T. A. (1977). Peel, Rowan and Mayne: The British model of urban police. In P. J. Stead (Ed.), *Pioneers in policing*. Maidenhead: McGraw Hill.

De Camargo, C. R. (2016). *A uniform not uniform: An ethnography of police clothing, performance, gender and subculture in neighbourhood policing*. University of Salford, PhD Thesis.

Devereaux, S. (2001). Before the Bobbies: The night watch and police reform in metropolitan London, 1720–1830. *Journal of British Studies, 40*(1), 146–152.

Dodd, V. (2018). UK police chiefs discuss officers routinely carrying guns. *The Guardian*, 17 May.

Edwards, C. J. (1999). *Changing policing theories: For 21st century societies*. Leichhardt, NSW: Federation Press.

Equality and Human Rights Commission. (2019). *Article 2: Right to life*. Available at: https://www.equalityhumanrights.com/en/human-rights-act/article-2-right-life.

Eustachewich, L. (2018), Knife attacks and murders spike in the UK. *New York Post*, 19 July.

Farmer, C., & Evans, R. (2019). Primed and ready: Does arming police increase safety? Preliminary findings. *Violence and Gender, 7*(2), 47–56 (Special Issue on Gun Violence).

Guardian. (2019). New Zealand police to start armed patrols after Christchurch massacre. *The Guardian*, 18 Oct.

Hendy, R. (2014). Routinely armed and unarmed police: What can the Scandinavian experience teach us? *Policing: A Journal of Policy and Practice, 8*, 183–192.

Heslop, R. (2015). The contribution of David H. Bayley, policing research pioneer. *Police Practice and Research, 16*, 512–526.

Hirschfield, P. J., & Simon, D. (2010). Legitimating police violence: Newspaper narratives of deadly force. *Theoretical Criminology, 14*, 155–182.

Home Office (UK). (2012). *Definition of policing by consent.* Available at: https://www.gov.uk/gov ernment/publications/policing-by-consent/definition-of-policing-by-consent.

Huq, A. Z., Jackson, J., & Trinkner, R. (2017). Legitimating practices: Revisiting the predicates of police legitimacy. *British Journal of Criminology, 57*(5), 1101–1122.

Ignatieff, M. (1979). The police and the people: The birth of Mr Peel's blue Locusts. *New Society, 3*, 443–445.

Knutsson, J., & Kuhns, J. B. (2010). *Police use of force: A global perspective.* Santa Barbara, California: Praeger.

Lentz, S. A., & Chaires, R. H. (2007). The invention of Peel's principles: A study of policing 'textbook' history. *Journal of Criminal Justice, 35*, 69–79.

Manning, P. (2012). Trust and accountability in Ireland: The case of An Garda Síochána. *Policing and Society, 22*, 346–361.

McNiffe, L. (1997). *A history of the Garda Síochána: A social history of the force 1922–52, with an overview of the years 1952–97.* Dublin: Wolfhound Press.

Morrison, G. B., & Vila, B. J. (1998). Police handgun qualification: Practical measure or aimless activity? *Policing, 21*, 510.

Mulroe, P. (2016). Policing twentieth century Ireland: A history of An Garda Siochana. *Irish Political Studies, 31*, 336–339.

O'Sullivan, N. (2015). Building trust and confidence—challenges and opportunities for the Garda Síochána. *Irish Probation Journal, 12*, 7–21.

Palmer, D. (2017), Police and policing. In D. Dalton, W. De Lint & Palmer, D. (Eds.), *Crime and justice: A guide to criminology*, 5th ed., Pyrmont, NSW: Thomson Reuters.

Palmer, S. H. (1988). *Police and protest in England and Ireland, 1780–1850.* Cambridge: Cambridge University Press.

Police News. (2010). Police Association conference calls for general arming of police. *Police News, 43*, 272. Published by the NZPA.

Police News. (2019). Tactical options high priority. *Police News,* Nov 12.

Reith, C. (1948). *A short history of the British police.* London: Oxford University Press.

Reith, C. (1952). *The blind eye of history: A study of the origins of the present police era.* London: Faber & Faber.

Rogers, M. D. (2003). Police force—an examination of the use of force, firearms and less-lethal weapons by British police. *Police Journal, 3*, 189–203.

Skolnick, J. H., & Fyfe, J. J. (1993). *Above the Law: Police and the excessive use of force.* Free Press: New York.

Squires, P., & Kennison, P. (2010). *Shooting to kill? Policing, firearms and armed response.* Chichester: Wiley.

Storch, R. D. (1975). The plague of the blue locusts: Police reform and popular resistance in northern england, 1840–57. *International Review of Social History, 20*, 61–90.

Taylor, D. N. (1997). *The New Police in nineteenth-century England: Crime, conflict, and control.* Manchester: Manchester University Press.

Tyler, T. R. (2006). *Why people obey the law.* Princeton, NJ: Princeton University Press.

Tyler, T. R., & Jackson, J. (2014). Popular legitimacy and the exercise of legal authority: Motivating compliance, cooperation, and engagement. *Psychology, Public Policy, and Law, 20*, 78–95.

Tyler, T. R., & Wakslak, C. J. (2004). Profiling and police legitimacy: Procedural justice, attributions of motive, and acceptance of police authority. *Criminology, 4*(2), 253–282.

United Nations. (1979). *Code of conduct for law enforcement officials.* New York: United Nations.

Victoria Police. (2003). *Victoria Police manual.* Melbourne: Victoria Police.

Victoria Police. (2014). *Victoria Police blue paper: A vision for Victoria Police in 2025.* Melbourne: Victoria Police.

Waldren, M. (2007). The arming of police officers. *Policing: A Journal of Policy and Practice, 1*, 255–264.

Chapter 4
'As Well Armed as the Criminal': The Armed Tradition

Abstract Contrasting with the doctrine of minimum force policing is the armed tradition of policing, which is explored in this chapter. In the Anglophone world, the armed tradition has two major streams. One derives from the centralised, mounted constabulary model widely used in the British Empire in colonial times. The other emerged from the community-based and less-disciplined policing services of the United States. In recent years the influence of the American armed tradition has become more widespread, a trend often referred to as militarisation. We use an Australian police organisation as a case study in how militarisation has led to changes in the uniforms and equipment of operational police. We also use American professional policing journals to interrogate the assumptions which underpin the armed tradition, particularly that police require powerful firearms, both to protect the community and to be safe themselves. We find a paucity of both coherent theory and real-world evidence to support these assumptions. We conclude that, as is true of the minimum force doctrine, the armed tradition of policing needs to be tested against evidence.

4.1 Introduction

In the majority of nations, police officers carry firearms as a matter of course; the armed tradition is both an operational norm and established community expectation. Only 19 countries currently do not deploy routinely armed police (University of Sydney 2019). Prominent among these are Great Britain, New Zealand, Ireland, Iceland, Norway, Botswana, Malawi, and a number of smaller Pacific island nations including Samoa, Nauru, Tonga and Fiji. Even in these routinely unarmed jurisdictions, specialist armed response units are increasingly normalised.

The great champion of the unarmed, minimum-force tradition of British policing, Charles Reith, does not trouble to conceal his scorn for American policing. Writing in 1952, he is scathing of the:

> … clumsiness and crudity of [American] police methods. Both police and criminals carry arms, and their contacts with each other very frequently take the form of shooting matches,

each side believing that, because the other side is armed, firing is necessary, in self-defence. Ignorance of the science of police tactics is never more clearly visible in American than in police handling of crowds, peaceful or unruly. (Reith 1952: 107)

To Reith, the aggressive demeanour and ready use of weapons by American police is an expression, not of strength but of weakness (Reith 1952: 107). Yet it is this approach to policing which dominates public debates in our own time. In the past thirty years, police in many jurisdictions (including those included within our comparative study, set out in Chaps. 5 and 6) have become increasingly militarised in their uniform, equipment and demeanour. This trend has been the subject of comment and concern among criminologists (see, for example, Insler et al. 2019; McCulloch 2001; Roziere and Walby 2018), but this concern has had little impact outside the academy. Arming police, making their weapons more numerous and more visible, and adopting uniforms with a military appearance, is said to be necessary in order to make communities safer. It is "common sense" that police, need to be armed. The implication is that a police officer without a gun is automatically helpless and ineffective (for a typical example, see Strandberg 2017).

This chapter explores the armed tradition of policing. We identify two streams within the armed tradition, one originating with the mounted constabularies of the British Empire, and the other arising from the more fragmented police organisations of the United States. We explore American-style militarisation, and argue that this approach to policing has become widely influential, using an Australian police organisation as a case study. We probe some of the assumptions underpinning the armed tradition. As is true of the minimum force doctrine, examined in Chap. 3, we find that the armed tradition is notable for a lack of coherent theory, and is even more bereft of supporting evidence.

4.2   The Armed Tradition in the United States

In the late 19th and early twentieth centuries, the United States faced the same challenges which had given rise to the Metropolitan Police in London. The rapid growth of urban centres was both facilitated by and necessary to the emerging industrialised factory system; however, it also broke down traditional forms of social control (Freeman 2018). Large scale migration from rural areas into cities frequently correlated with increased crime and disorder (King 2010). This was compounded in many American cities by the arrival of migrants from different cultures and ethnicities. In his pioneering study of youth gangs in Chicago in the 1920s, Thrasher documents gangs with origins in the city's Polish, Italian, Irish, Jewish, German, Swedish, Lithuanian and Czech communities (Thrasher 1963). The melting pot of America's burgeoning cities created problems of anti-social behaviour and crime beyond the capacity of existing forms of governance to manage (Miller 1975).

At the time, police forces in the United States were fragmented. Mostly small and under the control of local civic authorities, American police were often corrupt, ill-disciplined, and poorly armed (Brewer et al. 1996: 108–129). The late 19th and early twentieth century era of reform in the United States facilitated attempts to improve policing (Filler 1976). Figures such as August Vollmer attempted reform programs with familiar elements: lifting the social status of police, better pay and conditions, higher recruitment standards, stricter discipline, and so on (Carte and Flaine 1975). But while reformers were opposed to police brutality, a consistent theme was the need to make legitimate police violence more efficient and effective. If poorly-armed and ill-disciplined police were not able to fulfil their obligations, the argument went, then the solution was better weapons and improved training in how to use them (Chandler 1930). This philosophy was exemplified by George Fletcher Chandler, a 1920s police reformer, whose work with the police of New York State was regarded as a model for other jurisdictions:

> In the enforcement of law and order[,] history has shown that peace officers [*sic*: this term was often used interchangeably with "police officer" in this period] must sometimes use firearms … any arm that has been used under the rules of warfare may be used by the police. This includes revolvers, pistols, rifles of every description, tanks, machine guns, Gatling guns, gas, and even artillery … We feel that a firearm should be of the best manufacture and large enough to do any work required. Small calibre revolvers place the peace officer at a disadvantage, as he should be fully as well armed as the criminal. The same may be said of the rifle. Nothing less than the standard of the army … should be used. The rifle comes into use in rural districts in the hunting down of desperate criminals who are armed; or it may be used in riot duty.

> The revolver, we believe, should be at least a 0.38 caliber or more … and should be carried on the outside of the uniform in the place where it can most easily be drawn. There are two reasons why the revolver should be on the outside of the uniform: first, for the psychological effect, and secondly, because in the dangerous work of enforcing the law (and there is no more dangerous every-day work) a peace officer should have as good a chance as the criminal. What good, in an emergency, is a revolver in the hip-pocket under a heavy blouse and overcoat? Certainly no criminal would handicap himself as does the average police officer. (Chandler 1930: 44–45)

Chandler also stressed the importance of proper training, by which he meant training in marksmanship. Police who were unable to fire with good aim and to reload quickly were regarded as a liability. To this day, professional policing journals in the United States reflect Chandler's thinking. In response to police being targeted by offenders using high-powered rifles, the journal *Law Enforcement Technology* reported on "a nationwide debate about whether or not [police] departments are outgunned" (Strandberg 2017: 21).

> To be pinned down and helpless to shoot back effectively is a nightmare scenario for any law enforcement officer. But for many departments that's the reality, because their officers are solely equipped with department issued handguns, which are ineffective when shooting at longer range targets. Now some departments are taking action, including arming police officers with higher powered rifles, like the AR-15. (Strandberg 2017: 21)

A police union official is quoted:

> I absolutely think that we would be able to minimize the loss of life if our officers were better equipped... With these longer range weapons, we would be able to take out a threat from a longer distance. We would like to have the AR-15 … (Strandberg 2017: 23)

Another officer is paraphrased: "he felt that patrol cars needed to be equipped with high powered rifles, so that officers can defend themselves and their communities from attacks" (Strandberg 2017: 23).

The possible objections to this change in approach are summarised in less than a sentence: "Some politicians and community members don't want to see police officers with longer range rifles, as it brings to mind military or paramilitary forces …" (Strandberg 2017: 22). No other objection is raised, and no one taking this view is quoted directly. The article concludes:

> No reasonable person can argue that police officers need to be supplied with the proper tools to do their jobs. The challenge is to convince department administrations and the community at large that longer range rifles are needed. (Strandberg 2017: 23)

In the same journal, another author suggests that, to cut costs, police should learn to build their own AR-15 rifles from a kit: "I can get a complete gun of good quality for half the price of most other manufacturers' products. The product needs only a rear sight and is patrol-ready. Why not put an AR-15 into every patrol car in the agency?" (Bertomen 2014: 38). The rhetoric is all the more powerful for the gaps over which it glides: small calibre revolvers place the peace officer at a disadvantage; patrol cars needed to be equipped with high powered rifles, so that officers can defend themselves and their communities; why not put an AR-15 into every patrol car? No reasonable person can argue that police officers need to be supplied with the proper tools to do their jobs.

The unspoken assumption is that the *only* effective projection of police power is the firearm; it is "the proper tool", and any failure to fulfil the police mandate can be remedied by better and more powerful firearms. The enduring reality of Chandler's philosophy can be seen in the increase in the use of military grade equipment in many American police agencies. This equipment, often surplus material supplied by the armed forces under what is termed the "1033 program," includes machine guns, armoured vehicles, bayonets and grenade launchers (United States Government Accountability Office 2017; Delehanty et al. 2017). While acquiring such military equipment is a widespread trend, perhaps its most symbolic moment was the policing o f protests following the killing of an unarmed young black man in Ferguson, Missouri in 2014. As one observer put it:

> the police who faced protesters in Ferguson, Missouri looked more like soldiers than officers of the peace. Citizens squared off with a camouflage-clad police force armed with tear gas and grenade launchers, armored tactical vehicles and rifles with long-range scopes. (Rohde 2014)

4.3   The Armed Tradition and Police Use of Firearms

The armed tradition of policing takes a more pessimistic view of human nature and society than is the case with the minimum force doctrine. Recurring themes in the language used to justify the armed tradition are that it is a dangerous world, that community no longer functions to maintain order, and that criminals will use any and all weapons they are able to acquire in order to attain their vicious and desperate ends.

Echoing Chandler's concerns about insufficiently powerful weapons ("The revolver, we believe, should be at least a 0.38 caliber or more …") the rhetoric in American policing publications is one of perpetual concern; not about the harm firearms might do to people but the fear that *not enough harm* will be done (Bertomen 2015). The following is an extract from a product review, looking at a new model Glock automatic pistol:

> There are three factors which will stop the fight in an opponent. They can be stopped mechanically, psychologically, or physically. The 0.38 Long Colt was not enough. The 45 ACP [Automatic Colt Pistol] was. The 45 GAP [GLOCK Auto Pistol] is the just an updated version. Stopping a suspect psychologically does not require an effective firearm, or a firearm at all. It just needs to be a factor that strips the suspect of the will to fight. Stopping a suspect physically is different. If the suspect has a strong will to cause injury to an officer, they will continue to assault the officer long after a serious and sometimes fatal injury has been inflicted.
>
> One time I broke a bone on a suspect while engaged in a fight. He didn't even pay attention to it, intent on hurting me. I have talked to several officers who have hit a vital area of a suspect who attacked them with a lethal force. In each case, the wound to the suspect was fatal, but not immediately fatal. In one case, a suspect fired several rounds at the officer, missing him. The officer returned fire. One round struck the suspect's heart. He ran full speed for *almost a mile* before collapsing. In this case, the suspect must be stopped mechanically. That is, a bullet must stop the central nervous system or make the suspect mechanically unable to continue.
>
> I'm not saying that the 11 mm caliber is the answer to everything. It is just something that *may* increase the likelihood of success. (Bertomen 2015: 35)

It needs to be stressed that these words are not those of a wannabe military fantasist. The author, Lindsey Bertomen, is a former police officer who teaches Administration of Justice at Hartnell College, in Salinas, California (Hartnell College 2020). Bertomen's approach to firearms training claims to be scientific and, in a sense, it is. For example:

> 93 percent of the homicides on law enforcement officers involved a firearm in the past three years. More than 50 percent of these officers were shot within 5 feet — the remaining majority took place within 10 feet … How can we use these statistics to benefit our training? First, we should consider how some of the best competitive shooters in the world view their training philosophy. They learn to shoot a lot of bullets in a short time, then work on accuracy … it makes more sense to have the body and firearm deliver a clean shot, then align that clean shot to a good sight picture than the other way around. If the officer gets a good sight alignment and tries to chase it with a clean trigger break, the shot will be flawed. Officers should shoot a lot of bullets in order to learn to get the gun out of the holster and on target quickly. Once on target, officers should shoot until the threat is down. Pouring out a sufficient number of hits is good practice. (Bertomen, 2008: 84)

A sub-title in the article sums up the philosophy: "Shoot a lot of bullets". The possibility of injuring or killing someone who is not a dangerous offender, or not an offender at all, simply does not arise. This might seem like an extreme example of the armed tradition's philosophy, and doubtless there are many American police agencies and serving officers with a more restrained approach. However, the real-world experience of police shootings of civilians in the United States demonstrates that Bertomen's is not a rogue voice.

There is no reliable measure of deaths attributed to US police activity. A 2015 US Bureau of Justice Statistics review of its Arrest Related Deaths (ADR) dataset found a "significant underestimate of the annual number of arrest-related deaths" and that the ADR figure represented only "about 50% of the estimated law enforcement homicides" (Planty et al. 2015: 1). Even relying on ADR, the recorded number of civilians killed by police is far greater, both absolutely and in proportion to population, than in any comparable country (Evans et al. 2016). ADR-recorded "homicide—law enforcement" deaths in the period 2003–2009 totalled 2931, ranging from a high of 497 in 2009 to a "low" 376 in 2003 (Burch 2011). It is unclear what percentage of these deaths were the result of police use of firearms, but it is likely to be the great majority. FBI data records 2256 "justifiable homicide, law enforcement" deaths in the period 2013–2017: all but 17 of these deaths are attributed to firearms (Federal Bureau of Investigation 2017).

Zimring (2017) highlights the extremely unsatisfactory state of data on police killings in the United States and, having made a detailed study of the available information sources, arrives at a dramatic bottom line: "the annual death toll from police activity in the United states is well over 1000 civilians each year—three killings a day" (Zimring 2017: 24). Zimring also notes a lack of consciousness regarding the cost, both human and financial, of police shootings. The very terminology used in FBI data, "The killing of a felon by a law enforcement officer in the line of duty" (Federal Bureau of Investigation 2017) makes a rhetorical assertion and a value judgment. No auditing is undertaken to assess whether a particular death caused by police was indeed justified: it is merely assumed. The label "supports the claim that the killing of a felon is not a regrettable event," (Zimring 2017: 122). There are, therefore, no costs and the outcome is inherently positive.

Zimring also suggests that a great many deaths caused by police are not genuinely justified, but rather a result of the uncritical adoption of the American armed tradition, dressed up as science but never adequately tested. He gives the example of the "twenty-one-foot rule":

> For more than thirty years, police safety training has frequently included demonstrations that police confronted by persons lunging toward them with knives or other cutting instruments must start shooting their attackers when the attacking distance closes to twenty-one feet. (Zimring 2017: 100)

This principle originated in 1983 with John Tueller, a police firearms instructor in Salt Lake City, Utah. Tueller conducted some tests, and concluded that it was possible for a suspect armed with an edged weapon to fatally engage a police officer armed with a handgun within a distance of 21 feet (Martinelli 2014). From this, the "twenty-one-foot rule was born," and it spread to become both conventional wisdom and a standard protocol taught in training in law enforcement in the United States (Martinelli 2014). The twenty-one-foot rule became influential in other jurisdictions, including Canada (Gillis 2016). However, while the rule has since been discredited in Canada and is no longer taught to police, it remains a dominant teaching concept in the United States (Mann 2017).

The protocol has never been assessed in the United States, and there is no evidence to support it. A study of every American law enforcement fatality in the period 2008–2013, found that only two were due to knife wounds, and in both cases the weapons were small, concealed and used at very close range. The number of police fatalities resulting from people brandishing knives and lunging from a distance was zero (Zimring 2017: 101). Yet, the belief in the twenty-one-foot rule is so entrenched that it is invoked by police as a defence in court cases, and is cited in coronial inquests as an authoritative assessment of risk (Mann 2017; Gillis 2016).

America is, of course, a special case. The ubiquity of firearms in the community, including powerful military-grade weapons, makes policing there qualitatively different: "firearms in civilian hands are the elephant in the living room of what sets the United States apart from the rest of the developed world in violence against police as well as why U.S police kill civilians so often" (Zimring 2017: 88). In their international comparative analysis of the lethal use of firearms by police, Osso and Cano find that the United States is what might be called a "First World outlier", with both numbers and rates of killings by police far greater than Chile or the Russian Federation (Osse and Cano 2017: 641). It is for this reason that we decided not to include the US within the comparative analyses set out in Chap. 6 of this book. However, perhaps because of the enormous influence of American popular culture on most of the Anglophone world (which we examine in Chap. 7), the appearance and equipment worn by police in other countries has for many years increasingly reflected the US armed tradition.

4.4 The Spread of the Armed Tradition

Central to the armed tradition of policing is the gun. Bittner (1975) joins many scholars of American policing to remark on the poor quality of police firearms training, but adds: "All of this is of slight importance … because in the United States the pistol is not mainly a tool but an emblem the symbolic value of which draws on history and myth" (Bittner 1975: 101). The armed policeman in America, he argues, reflects both the popular interest in arms and the symbolic gesture that the drawn gun has in folklore, games, fiction, and reality. A police officer who is unarmed is defenceless, ineffective—not, indeed, a police officer at all. The gun is the essence of policing (Bittner 1975: 102).

Such symbolism has become near ubiquitous. Figure 4.1 illustrates the point. The image shows a children's toy set, manufactured in China and intended for wide international sale (this example was purchased in Australia, but the safety warnings are printed in three languages). The set, called "Official Police Play," comprises a watch, a riot shield, a baton and—most prominently—a gun (Official Police Play 2012). It might seem overly politically-correct to object to a child's toy set, but it is

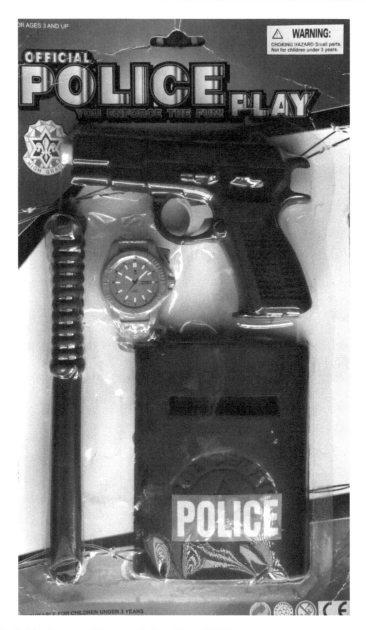

Fig. 4.1 Children's toy set (Photograph: Rose Evans 2020)

symbolic of the core association in the American armed tradition, which is a relatively recent development outside the United States.

Historically, as former British settler colonies, Canada, New Zealand and Australia have all followed a mix of two British policing models. One was the unarmed minimum-force urban policing of the New Police, discussed in Chap. 3. The other was the armed and mounted quasi-military force; first developed in Ireland as the Royal Irish Constabulary (RIC), it was later adopted across many parts of the British Empire where the population was, like the Irish, considered of doubtful loyalty (Tobias 1977). The administration of what were initially thinly-populated colonial societies, in which the indigenous people were regarded with varying degrees of prejudice and hostility, required a centrally-controlled, armed police force based on the RIC model. The North West Mounted Police, later the Royal Canadian Mounted Police, was one example (Morton 2006, 2018). New Zealand and each of the colonies which later formed Australia, all introduced armed and mounted constabularies in the late nineteenth century (O'Sullivan 1978; Haldane 1986; Johnston 1992; Conole 2002; Macleod 1997; Roth 1998). Members of one such corps are the "troopers, one, two, three", mentioned in Australia's de facto national song, "Waltzing Matilda" (Richardson 2006).

It is beyond the scope of this book to examine the many variations in the implementation and experience of the RIC policing model across the British Empire. However, two points are worth stressing. First, while the RIC model did involve the routine arming of police, it also emphasised central control of and personal discipline among officers (Conole 2002; Evans 2005; Haldane 1986; Johnston 1992; Tobias 1977). It is necessary to stress that this relatively benign picture of British Imperial mounted constabularies was racially exclusive. In some colonies, including Queensland, mounted police were at times agents of genocidal violence (see, for example, Moody 2019). Second, while mounted constabularies were widespread, in those parts of the Empire where there were significant white settler populations, there was awareness of and pressure for the unarmed London Metropolitan Police model of policing.

Australia provides a case study for how the two models conjoined. The administration of sparsely-populated communities in which the indigenous people were regarded with prejudice and hostility, required a centrally-controlled, armed police force, and the RIC model persisted in some areas well into the twentieth century (Conole 2002; Johnston 1992). However, as Australian society became more urban the minimum-force model became more dominant, at least in cities and larger towns (Evans 2005; Haldane 1986). One legacy of the RIC model was a high level of centralisation (each state and territory has one centralised police service) which has been criticised for distancing police from local communities, and fostering a hierarchical and bureaucratic organisation (Finnane 1994).

It would be inaccurate to suggest that Australian policing developed in a homogeneous manner. States and territories adopted and developed different approaches to policing and the use of firearms. Some jurisdictions, such as New South Wales and Queensland, have routinely armed police since colonial times (Hoban 1962; Johnston 1992) but, at least in urban areas, weapons were carried discretely and used rarely (Haldane 1986). There were notorious incidents of police violence, such as the Rothbury shooting of 1929, in which police guarding a coal mine fired on picketing miners, killing one man (Evans 2012). However, the Rothbury incident appalled the community precisely because it was so unexpected. Even labour leaders at the time were at pains to emphasise that the New South Wales Police were known for their tact and ability to keep the peace, even in trying circumstances such as industrial disputes.

4.5 A Case Study in Weaponisation: Victoria Police

Since the 1980s, Australian policing has become increasingly weaponised. This is particularly true of the state of Victoria, where the appearance of routine operational police has changed markedly. Victoria has traditionally regarded itself as a peaceful and harmonious community, and its police enjoy a generally good reputation for integrity and competence. A semi-official history of Victoria Police was titled *The People's Force*, and there is some truth to this description (Haldane 1986). Scandals over corruption and misconduct occur, and indeed recur (Office of Police Integrity (Victoria) 2007). An external integrity agency, the Independent Broad-based Anti-Corruption Commission (IBAC) writes: "The Victorian community rightly expects that its police officers will perform their duties and exercise their significant powers (including the power to detain, search and arrest, and use force) fairly, impartially and in accordance with the law" (IBAC 2016: 5). This quote comes from an investigation which found that police had not, in fact, lived up to these standards: nonetheless, this community expectation is usually met.

Historically, police on ordinary duty in Victoria did not carry firearms at all, though detectives were routinely armed. Beginning in the 1970s, uniformed police were deployed equipped with a semi-automatic pistol, usually carried concealed under the uniform jacket. In 1979, Victoria Police began carrying a Smith & Wesson revolver, which was too bulky to carry in a concealed manner. By the mid-1980s, uniform officers were routinely equipped with a revolver housed in a waist holster (McCulloch 2001).

In the same period, the Victorian community was shocked by several incidents in which police were killed or seriously wounded, including by a car bomb planted outside police headquarters and the assassination-style murder of two police officers. These incidents overlapped with two mass-shootings in which high-powered rifles were used. Though the mass shootings were not targeted specifically at police, taken together these incidents of extreme violence contributed to a heightened sense of vulnerability among police (Victoria Police 1995). Victoria Police responded with training focussed on firearms and defensive physical tactics; there was little or no training in controlling violence without physical confrontation, or understanding and dealing with people affected by mental illness (Office of Police Integrity (Victoria) 2005). The number of civilians killed by police firearms in Victoria, already high, continued to rise. Between 1984 and 1995, 35 people were shot dead by Victoria

Police officers, more than twice as many as all the other Australian jurisdictions combined. Most of those killed were mentally ill, and committing only minor offences (Saligari and Evans 2015).

Alarm over the number of deaths prompted Victoria Police to reassess officer training. An internal inquiry led to a change of philosophy and training under the banner Operation Beacon. Introduced in 1994, Operation Beacon emphasised a "safety-first" philosophy, embracing the safety of police and the wider community, as well as suspects (Victoria Police 2003: Instruction 101–101.104). The key message of Operation Beacon was that "the success of an operation will primarily be judged by the extent to which the use of force is avoided or minimised" (Victoria Police 2003). The program appeared to be effective: 32 people were fatally shot by Victoria Police in the 12 years prior to Project Beacon; this number fell to 16 in the subsequent 12 years (Kesic et al. 2010). However, of concern was that the rate of deaths was increasing again: there were six fatalities in the period January 2003—May 2005. This spike caused an external agency, the Office of Police Integrity (OPI), to conduct a review which found that "policy, practices and procedures [i.e. Operation Beacon] have remained unchanged but the requisite ongoing and continuous attention to use of force issues as part of the planning decision-making of Victoria Police has fallen away"(Office of Police Integrity (Victoria) 2005: 55). In one high profile case, a 15-year-old boy, Tyler Cassidy, was shot dead by police officers 73 s after they made initial contact with him (State Coroner (Vic) 2011). External reviews again criticised the tendency for officers to resolve incidents quickly, and for police training to focus on equipment and hands-on tactics rather than communication skills (Office of Police Integrity (Victoria) 2009).

Rogers (2003) notes that in Britain sentiment towards arming police tends to be reactive: if armed police kill a non-offender, concern about armed police increases; conversely, if unarmed police fail to prevent a tragedy there can be pressure for increased police access to firearms. This pattern is also evident in Australia. In recent years there have been incidents in which offenders have murdered other citizens, and police have been criticised for not using lethal force earlier. Notable examples include the 2014 Lindt Café siege in Sydney (a lone-wolf terrorist action), and the 2017 Bourke Street massacre in Melbourne, in which a man wanted for attempted murder was monitored but not apprehended, and eventually drove a vehicle into pedestrians in a shopping precinct, killing six people (State Coroner (NSW) 2017; Tran 2020).

Though the Lindt café siege occurred outside Victoria, both events prompted Victoria Police to promise a more aggressive approach to threatening situations (Goldsworthy 2019). In 2017, a review by a state government-appointed Expert Panel on Terrorism recommended changes to legislation to clarify that "a police officer … may use force, including pre-emptive lethal force, against a person who the police officer … believes on reasonable grounds is likely to commit an indictable offence that will cause serious injury to, or the death of, another person" (Department of Premier and Cabinet (Victoria) 2017: 7). This recommendation was implemented. Operation Beacon's "safety first" principles were formally replaced with a plan to "reduce the number of casualties rather than engineer a peaceful resolution" (Sylvester 2017).

The new Operational Response Principles empowered the first officers on the scene to take "instant action" if lives were at risk. A Deputy Commissioner told media that police would "always try to use minimum force", but "changing threats" meant that officers needed to be trained to deal with "the mentally ill, drug affected, terror suspects and active armed offenders" (Sylvester 2017).

In 2019, Victoria Police announced the purchase of 600 AR-15 automatic rifles, with 800 officers to be trained in their use (Neville 2019). The justification offered by the incumbent Police Minister is straight from the armed tradition: "We're giving police the powers, tools and resources they need to tackle emerging risks … we'll continue to give police the tools they need to keep the community safe" (Neville 2019). The main specialist unit to use the rifles, the Public Order Response Team, also acquired a range of other new weapons, including semi-automatic pepper-ball rifles which fire capsicum rounds, launchers which fire rubber bullets, stinger grenades and "flash/noise distraction devices designed to shock and disperse violent crowds" (Sylvester 2019).

The gradual shift in approach by Victoria Police, from a clear minimum-force doctrine to a version of the armed tradition can be traced in the pages of its official publication, *Police Life*. Such publications are useful to researchers because they show how an organisation, or at least those with power and influence within it, wish to be perceived. First published in 1958, *Police Life* has evolved from a newspaper format to a glossy magazine, published quarterly. Since 2008, the publication has also been available online (Victoria Police 2020). Like many corporate publications, *Police Life* has two overlapping aims: to boost morale and institutional pride among staff, and to improve the image of Victoria Police among the wider community. Unsurprisingly, *Police Life* reflects many of the tensions and contradictions faced by modern police organisations (Manning 2014). Are we a force, or a service? Are we here to help the vulnerable and engage with the community, or are we strong, determined law enforcers?

Since the 1980s, *Police Life* has focused on inclusion and community policing. In any given issue, there are pictures of police officers out on the roads and in a range of public places, keeping the peace at demonstrations, chatting to members of the community or visiting homes (Police Life 2012a, 2013, 2016a, 2017a, b). A perennial theme is recognition that Victoria's community is multi-cultural, and increasingly so, and that this requires greater awareness by and training of police, along with diverse recruitment, so that Victoria Police has a workforce which represents its community (Police Life 1985a, 1985b, 1986, 1996, 1999a, b, 2000, 2004, 2006).

The police depicted in *Police Life* photographs are usually wearing uniform. From the 1970s, *Police Life* shows officers in a uniform of royal blue trousers and jacket, with a light blue shirt. The style of headwear changes, from a peaked cap to a broad-brimmed hat, then to a baseball-style cap. From the 1980s a visible sidearm is carried on the hip, but in the minimum-force tradition it is clearly a non-military uniform. However, in the past twenty years, the look of police has become steadily more military, and the weaponry carried has become more obvious. In 2013 comes a big shift: the standard uniform changes to a much darker navy blue, almost black (Police Life 2013). There is no contrast: every item of the uniform is the same dark colour.

Officers on patrol wear a ballistics vest, and have an automatic pistol strapped to the thigh (Police Life 2013). From 2014, most operational officers are also equipped with conducted energy devices (Cooper 2014).

The friendly community police officer remains an ideal, but that role has become increasingly incongruous, at odds with the uniform. Across the pages of *Police Life* officers are still depicted smiling, talking to members of a migrant community, sitting at a kitchen table reassuring a woman experiencing family violence, or strolling with a woman leading a horse near a rural police station (see, for example, Police Life 2012a,2016a,2017a; b). However, there is a growing disjunct between the role the police perform, the semi-military apparel they wear, and the visible firearms they carry.

Much more than is the case in previous decades, *Police Life* increasingly depicts officers in confrontational or militaristic poses, and guns are more often seen drawn and aimed. Figure 4.2 illustrates the change. On the left is part of a cover image from 2010, the friendly community police officer (Police Life 2010: 1). On the right is an image from 2017. A figure armed with a rifle and wearing combat fatigues is shown in silhouette: he could be a soldier (Police Life 2017c: 1). Other recent images include an officer crouched on one knee aiming his semi-automatic pistol (Police Life 2016b: 1); helmeted police with rifles and gas masks poised for action in a corridor (Police Life 2012b: 24), or peering cautiously around a corner, automatic pistols raised (Police Life 2018: 11). A full-page advertisement in a special "recruitment edition" invites applicants to be "a force for good". We see two police from the back,

Fig. 4.2 Victoria Police as depicted on the cover of *Police Life* (Left-hand image Spring 2010; right-hand image Spring 2017). Permission to use images granted by Victoria Police

one female and one male, wearing ballistics vests and carrying firearms. The picture is dark, tense. There are no members of the community shown, just a police car, also dark blue (Police Life 2017d: 32). Lots of equipment; visible weapons; no people.

The image which sums up this transition is a picture, Fig. 4.3, intended for primary school-age children to colour in. The image shows a little girl standing happily next to two police officers. Both have a semi-automatic pistol strapped to their thighs (Police Life 2018). This is the understanding of policing exemplified by the "Official Police Play" toy set depicted in Fig. 4.1 (Official Police Play 2012). From the earliest age, Victorian children are taught that a gun is central to, and a key identifying feature of, being a police officer. This is the armed tradition, becoming engrained, and becoming normalised.

Victoria Police provides a case study of a police organisation which was founded on the armed, centralised model of the RIC, shifting with increased urbanisation to embrace the minimum force doctrine, and then shifting again: this time towards the more aggressive American armed tradition, in which a firearm is central to the very idea of policing.

It might be asked, then, why we have not included Melbourne, the capital city of Victoria, in our study (set out in Chaps. 5 and 6). This was, in fact, the original idea underpinning this project. The reason we did not use Melbourne as an example is the lack of comparable jurisdictions. In June 2019, Melbourne had a population of 5.1 million people (ABS 2020). This is an unusual size. Other cities which might be used for comparison are either much larger (such as London, 8.9 million or New York City, 8.6 million) or much smaller (Berlin 3.7 million, Paris 2.1 million, Toronto 2.9 million). If it were located in the United States, Melbourne would be the second largest city in the country, well ahead of Los Angeles (4 million) or Chicago (2.7 million). The only comparable First World city is Sydney, population 5.3 million, but that city is also in Australia and is also a routinely-armed jurisdiction. We wished to compare routinely-armed and routinely-unarmed policing, and the effect it has on the safety of both police officers and the community, in locations which were as similar as possible. That is why, for the purposes of our comparative analysis, the city of Brisbane (population 2.3 million) was chosen as the Australian location.

4.6   Chapter Conclusion

The increased adoption of the armed tradition by police in Victoria has attracted little adverse comment and, indeed, very little debate at all. It is widely seen as necessary, inevitable, and at its core a good thing: "we'll continue to give police the tools they need to keep the community safe" (Neville 2019); "Police to get high-powered guns in drive to sweep terror off streets" (Sylvester 2019); "We are looking at the current environment in Victoria and across the nation and if we need to enhance what we provide our members [i.e. police] we will" (Rizmal 2018). More, and more powerful, weapons will, goes the underlying assumption, keep safe the people who keep us safe.

Fig. 4.3 A Victoria Police children's colouring sheet, promoting police-community relations (*Police Life*, Summer 2018: 17). Permission to use image granted by Victoria Police

But is this true? As Zimring (2017) remarks in relation to the twenty-one-foot rule examined earlier in this chapter, there is a clear need "that statistics and analysis about the actual risk to police from different kinds of violent assaults becomes an important part of the analysis and evaluation of police use of deadly force" (Zimring 2017: 102). Do armed police make the community safer? Do they make police themselves safer? In the next two chapters, we seek to provide statistical rather than rhetorical answers to these questions.

Acknowledgements We thank Victoria Police for granting permission to use images from *Police Life* magazine in this chapter.

References

Bertomen, L. (2008). Statistically, you're correct. *Law Enforcement Technology, 35,* 80–85.

Bertomen, L. (2014). Building an AR-15. *Law Enforcement Technology, 41,* 34–38.

Bertomen, L. (2015). Inside Glock's 38: Something for every day of the week. *Law Enforcement Technology, 42,* 30–35.

Bittner, E. (1975). *The functions of the police in modern society: A review of background factors, current practices, and possible role models.* New York: Jason Aronson.

Brewer, J. D., Guelke, A., Hume, I., et al. (1996). *he police, public order and the state: Policing in Great Britain, Northern Ireland, the Irish Republic, the USA, Israel, South Africa and China.* Basingstoke: Macmillan.

Burch, A. M. (2011). Arrest-related deaths, 2003–2009—statistical tables. *Bureau of Justice Statistics* [https://www.bjs.gov/]. Washington, DC: Bureau of Justice Statistics.

Australian Bureau of Statistics. (2020). *Regional population statistics: About the population and components of change (births, deaths, migration) for Australia's capital cities and regions.* Available at: https://www.abs.gov.au/statistics/people/population/regional-population/2018-19.

Carte, G. E., & Flaine, H. C. (1975). *Police Reform in the United States: The Era of August Vollmer,* 1905–1932. Berkeley: University of California Press.

Chandler, G. F. (1930). *The policeman's manual: A standard guide to the latest methods and duties of American police.* New York: Funk & Wagnalls.

Conole, P. (2002). *Protect and serve: A history of policing in Western Australia.* Perth, WA: Western Australia Police Service.

Cooper, M. (2014). 580 police Tasers to hit the streets across Victoria. *The Age* [Melbourne], 23 Apr.

Delehanty, C., Mewhirter, J., & Welch, R., et al. (2017). Militarization and police violence: The case of the 1033 program. *Research and Politics, 4*(2). https://doi.org/10.1177/2053168017712885.

Department of Premier and Cabinet (Victoria). (2017). *Expert panel on terrorism and violent extremism prevention and response powers: Report 1.* Werribee: Victorian Government Library Service.

Evans, R. W. (2005). William John Mackay and the New South Wales Police Force, 1910–1948: A study of police power, PhD thesis. *School of Political and Social Inquiry,* Monash University, Melbourne.

Evans, R., (2012). "'Murderous coppers': Police, industrial disputes and the 1929 rothbury shootings." *History Australia 9*(1), 176–200.

Evans, R., Farmer, C., & Saligari, J. (2016). Mental illness and gun violence: Lessons for the United States from Australia and Britain. *Violence and Gender, 3,* 150–156.

Federal Bureau of Investigation. (2017). *Expanded homicide data table 14: Justifiable homicide by weapon, law enforcement, 2013–2017.* Available at: https://ucr.fbi.gov/crime-in-the-u.s/2017/crime-in-the-u.s.-2017/tables/expanded-homicide-data-table-14.xls.

Filler, L. (1976). *The Muckrakers.* University Park, PA: Pennsylvania State University Press.

Finnane, M. (1994). *Police and government: Histories of policing in Australia.* Melbourne: Oxford University Press.

Freeman, J. B. (2018). *Behemoth: A history of the factory and the making of the modern world.* New York: W. W. Norton.

Gillis, W. (2016). 'Outdated' 21-foot rule for police shootings finally bites the dust. *Toronto Star,* 21 Mar.

Goldsworthy, T. (2019). Victorian police have 'shoot to kill' powers when cars are used as weapons: Here's why this matters. *The Conversation,* 28 Oct.

Haldane, R. (1986). *The people's force: A history of the Victoria Police.* Melbourne: Melbourne University Press.

Hartnell College [California]. (2020) *Hartnell employee directory.* Available at: https://www.hartnell.edu/directory.html.

Hoban, L. (1962). *New South Wales Police Force: 1862–1962.* Sydney: Government Printer.

Independent Broad-based Anti-Corruption Commission (IBAC). (2016). *Operation Ross: An investigation into police conduct in the Ballarat Police Service Area.* Melbourne: IBAC.

Insler, M. A., McMurrey, B., & McQuoid, A. F. (2019). From broken windows to broken bonds: Militarized police and social fragmentation. *Journal of Economic Behaviour & Organization, 163,* 43–62.

Johnston, W. R. (1992). *The long blue line: A history of the Queensland police.* Brisbane: Boolarong.

Kesic, D., Thomas, S. D. M., & Ogloff, J. R. P. (2010). Mental illness among police fatalities in Victoria 1982–2007: Case linkage study. *Australian & New Zealand Journal of Psychiatry, 44,* 463–468.

King, P. (2010). The impact of urbanization on murder rates and on the geography of homicide in England and Wales, 1780–1850. *The Historical Journal, 53,* 671.

Macleod, C. (1997). *Patrol in the Dreamtime.* Melbourne: Mandarin.

Mann, R. (2017). The 21-foot rule: Why is it important? *Shooting Illustrated,* 16 Oct.

Manning, P. K. (2014). Role and function of the police. In G. Bruinsma & D. Weisburd (Eds.), *Encyclopedia of criminology and criminal justice* (pp. 4510–4529). New York: Springer.

Martinelli, R. (2014). Revisiting the '21-foot-rule'. *Police Magazine,* 18 Sept.

McCulloch, J. (2001). *Blue army: Paramilitary policing in Australia.* Melbourne: Melbourne University Press.

Miller, W. R. (1975). Police authority in London and New York City 1830–1870. *Journal of Social History, 8,* 81–90.

Moody, G. (2019). Coming to terms with the brutal history of Queensland's Native Mounted Police. *ABC Radio National,* 24 Jul.

Morton, D. (2006). *A short history of Canada.* Toronto: McCelland & Stewart.

Morton, D. (2018). Cavalry or police: Keeping the peace on two adjacent frontiers, 1870–1900. *Journal of Canadian Studies/Revue D'études Canadiennes, 12,* 27–37.

Neville, L. (2019). *New police firepower to target major incidents,* Minister for Police and Emergency Services [media release], 17 February 2019. Available from: https://www.premier.vic.gov.au/wp-content/uploads/2019/02/190217-New-Police-Firepower-To-Target-Major-Incidents.pdf.

O'Sullivan, J. S. (1978). *Mounted police in NSW.* Adelaide: Rigby.

Office of Police Integrity (Victoria). (2005). *Review of fatal shootings by Victoria Police.* Melbourne: Office of Police Integrity.

Office of Police Integrity (Victoria). (2007). *Past patterns—future directions: Victoria Police and the problem of corruption and serious misconduct.* Melbourne: Office of Police Integrity.

Office of Police Integrity (Victoria). (2009). *Review of the use of force by and against Victoria Police.* Melbourne: Office of Police Integrity.

Official Police Play. (2012). Official police play [children's toy set]. China.

Osse, A., & Cano, I. (2017). Police deadly use of firearms: An international comparison. *International Journal of Human Rights, 21,* 629–649.

Planty, M., Burch, A. M., Banks, D., et al. (2015). *Arrest-related deaths program: Data quality profile.* Bureau of Justice Statistics (United States): Technical Report.

Police Life. (1985a). Breaking the language barrier. *Police Life,* Oct, 178.

Police Life. (1985b). The language lifeline. *Police Life,* Jun, 114.

Police Life. (1986). Vietnamese back police for community award. *Police Life,* Dec, 221.

Police Life. (1996). Kids in crisis. *Police Life,* Aug, 21.

Police Life. (1999a). Asian connection: Talking the talk takes on an entirely new meaning for police dealing with Victoria's Asian communities. *Police Life,* Sept, 22–23.

Police Life. (1999b). Meeting of the twain. *Police Life,* Jun, 7.

Police Life. (2000). A diverse workforce for a diverse community. *Police Life,* Mar, 34–35.

Police Life. (2004). Koran for oath of police. *Police Life,* Mar, 23.

Police Life. (2006). Taking a good look at themselves. *Police Life,* Oct, 28–29.

Police Life. (2010). *Police Life,* Spring: 1.

Police Life. (2012a). *Police Life,* Summer: 16–17.

Police Life. (2012b). *Police Life,* Winter: 16–17.

Police Life. (2013). *Police Life,* Winter: 16–17.

Police Life. (2016a). *Police Life,* Summer: 24.

Police Life. (2016b). *Police Life,* Spring: 24.

Police Life. (2017a). *Police Life,* Autumn: 17.

Police Life. (2017b). *Police Life,* Spring: 17.

Police Life. (2017c). *Police Life,* Summer: 1.

Police Life. (2017d). *Police Life,* Recruitment Edition: 17.

Police Life. (2018). *Police Life,* Summer: 17.

Reith, C. (1952). *The blind eye of history: A study of the origins of the present police era.* London: Faber & Faber.

Richardson, M. (2006). *Once a jolly swagman: The ballad of Waltzing Matilda.* Melbourne: Melbourne University Publishing.

Rizmal, Z. (2018). Victoria Police should 'resist the trend' towards militarisation with new powerful weapons. *ABC News,* 29 Mar.

Rogers, M. D. (2003). Police force—an examination of the use of force, firearms and less-lethal weapons by British Police. *Police Journal 76*(3), 189–203.

Rohde, J. (2014). Police militarization is a legacy of cold war paranoia. *The Conversation,* 22 Oct. Available from: https://theconversation.com/police-militarization-is-a-legacy-of-cold-war-paranoia-32251. Accessed 24 Feb 2019.

Roth, M. (1998). Mounted police forces: A comparative history. *Policing, 21*(4), 707–719.

Roziere, B., & Walby, K. (2018). The expansion and normalization of police militarization in Canada. *Critical Criminology, 26,* 29–48. https://doi.org/10.1007/s10612-017-9378-3.

Saligari, J., & Evans, R. W. (2015). Beacon of hope? Lessons learned from efforts to reduce civilian deaths from police shootings in an Australian state. *Journal of Urban Health* (First online). https://doi.org/10.1007/s11524-015-9996-6.

State Coroner (NSW). (2017). Inquest into the deaths arising from the Lindt Café siege: findings and recommendations. Sydney: State Coroner (NSW).

State Coroner (Vic). (2011). Redacted finding into death with inquest: Tyler Jordan Cassidy. Melbourne: Coroners Court of Victoria.

Strandberg, K. W. (2017). A call to arms. *Law Enforcement Technology, 44*(1), 20–23.

Sylvester, J. (2017). Police retrained to respond to terror threat. *The Age* [Melbourne], 11 Dec.

Sylvester, J. (2019). Police to get high-powered guns in drive to sweep terror off streets. *The Age* [Melbourne], 18 Dec.

Thrasher, F. M. (1963). *The gang: A study of 1,313 gangs in Chicago.* Chicago: University of Chicago Press.

Tobias, J. J. (1977). The British colonial police: An alternative police style. In P. J. Stead (Ed.), *Pioneers in Policing.* Maidenhead: McGraw Hill.

Tran, D. (2020). Families of Bourke Street attack victims tell coroner Victoria Police failed them. *ABC News* [Melbourne], 26 Feb.

United States Government Accountability Office. (2017). *DOD excess property: enhanced controls needed for access to excess controlled property* [GAO-17-532]. Washington, DC: Government Accountability Office.

University of Sydney (2019). *GunPolicy.org* [online]. University of Sydney. Available from: https://www.gunpolicy.org/about. Accessed 30 Nov 2019.

Victoria Police. (1995). *Project beacon: Overview of progress.* Melbourne: Victoria Police.

Victoria Police. (2003). *Victoria police manual.* Melbourne: Victoria Police.

Victoria Police. (2020) *Police Life magazine.* Available at: https://www.police.vic.gov.au/police-life-magazine.

Zimring, F. E. (2017). *When police kill.* Cambridge, Mass: Harvard University Press.

Chapter 5
Operationalising Minimum Force: The Need for Evidence

Abstract In Chaps. 3 and 4, we examined the minimum force and armed traditions of policing. We drew attention to key assumptions which frame support for both routinely armed and routinely unarmed policing, and highlighted the absence of empirical evidence to underpin any argument for change. In this chapter we introduce our comparative study, which set out to develop an evidence base to inform understanding of the effects on safety of the routine arming of police officers. We explain the rationale and research design for our study, the choice of four locations used in our analysis, and the ways in which minimum force is operationalised in each. We then document our research method and approach, and also acknowledge a number of methodological limitations.

5.1 Introduction

New Zealand and Great Britain are two of 19 countries which currently do not deploy routinely armed police (University of Sydney 2019).[1] Armed response provisions exist across both nations but, on a day to day basis, the majority of police officers patrol without carrying firearms.[2] In Great Britain, a number of high-profile incidents and perceived changes in criminal behaviour, such as a rise in random knife-crime, have contributed to a heightening of calls for more general arming of police (Dodd 2017, 2018; Eustachewich 2018; Robinson 2019). The March 2019 terror attack on a mosque in Christchurch triggered renewed discussion of the merits of routinely arming New Zealand's police officers (Menon 2019). Recent events have prompted restrained but tangible operational changes in both jurisdictions. Late in 2018, London's Metropolitan Police confirmed the deployment of routinely armed patrols in a number of high crime areas, with officers carrying their firearms visibly (Dodd 2018). In October 2019, a six-month trial of armed patrols was introduced in

---

[1] Prominent among the others are Ireland, Iceland, Norway, Botswana, Malawi, and a number of smaller island nations such as Samoa, Nauru, Tonga and Fiji.

[2] All New Zealand officers are trained to use firearms, and frontline police vehicles carry firearms in a lock box.

three locations across New Zealand. The Police Commissioner, Mike Bush, offered an assurance that the presence of armed police would enhance the safety of officers and the community.

> Following the events of March 15 [2019] in Christchurch, our operating environment has changed… Police must ensure our people are equipped and enabled to perform their roles safely and to ensure our communities are, and feel, safe. This means having the right people with the right tools, skills and knowledge ready to respond at all times… (Bush 2019)

Such an assertion is typical within the discourse of policing and firearms. A common-sense rhetoric underpins arguments for the need for police to be routinely armed—it is regarded by advocates as essential. Indeed, in a majority of international jurisdictions, the routine arming of police officers is an established and expected norm. This is, perhaps, the ultimate expression of reassurance policing (discussed in various contexts by, for example, Fielding and Innes 2006; Crawford 2017; Fleming 2005). The visible presence of armed police is argued by proponents to be inherently protective and comforting, and is presumed to act as a tangible deterrent to those intent on wrongdoing. The counter-implication is that a police officer without ready access to a gun is helpless and ineffective, a perspective aptly expressed by an ex-Metropolitan Police firearms officer:

> Your job is to protect the public. How can you do that if you cannot first protect yourself? (Long 2016)

However, there is little empirical evidence to support this contention, or to demonstrate that jurisdictions in which police are routinely armed are intrinsically safer (Farmer and Evans 2019). Rhetorical or presumption-driven justifications should not be sufficient for such a core aspect of policing. Such assertions also suggest a conceptual and operational dissonance when we consider how they coalesce and fit within the doctrine of minimum force which, as we explored in Chap. 2, is deeply engrained across policing scholarship and practice.

There is a need, therefore, for robust and ongoing analysis of the effects, on the use of force by police in general, and on measures of safety in particular, of the routine presence/absence of firearms. Rather than assuming an inevitable beneficence for either tradition, we argue for an evidence-based examination: to interrogate whether, and to what extent, the locations in which police are routinely armed are demonstrably safer. For example, are key measures of crime and criminality notably higher where police are not routinely armed? Is the risk or likelihood of being fatally shot by police consistent across comparable armed and unarmed jurisdictions? And what about the police themselves; are routinely armed police officers safer than those who do not carry firearms? There is insufficient evidence that the Christchurch mosque attack or any of the recent incidents in Great Britain would have been prevented by the police in those communities being armed. Indeed, in an independent assessment of responses to a series of attacks in London and Manchester between March and June 2017, David Anderson QC concluded that:

> *not everything can be stopped* … determined attackers will always have a chance of getting through… no responsible person could offer a copper-bottomed assurance that terrorists will

always be stopped. The same is of course true in relation to other types of crime. (Anderson 2017: 47 [emphasis in original])

It seems logical that the routine presence of firearms in any police interaction could increase the risk of their use, appropriate or otherwise. In light of renewed calls for the routine arming of frontline police officers, we have undertaken a comparative examination of four jurisdictions: two where police officers are routinely armed, and two where they are not. Our purpose is to explore the expectation that the routine arming of police officers correlates with improved levels of safety—for the community and for police officers themselves. The findings from our analysis are presented in Chap. 6 from the perspective of both community safety and police officer safety. In this chapter we set out the rationale for the study, including an explanation for the choice of locations, and we document provisions relating to the police use of force within the four jurisdictions. We explain the research approach that has been applied, and acknowledge a number of methodological limitations.

5.2 The Doctrine of Minimum Force

As we explored in Chap. 3, the doctrine of minimum force is deeply engrained across legal, conceptual and operational policing practice and procedures, and enshrined within international protocols such as the United Nations' Code of Conduct for Law Enforcement Officials. Policing texts and scholarly articles examining the police use of force routinely contain passages which set out the expectations of minimum force. Such statements are uncontroversial and unremarkable. They reflect an operational and philosophical imperative about which few politicians, media commentators, scholars of policing or police officers themselves are likely to object. The designation of "minimum" as a qualifying prefix in relation to permissible levels of force is ubiquitous within a research context, and across police procedures, use of force guidelines, firearms best practice, and legislative provisions. The over-riding expectation of minimum force is clear and conceptually consistent.

By contrast, the operationalisation of minimum force in the context of policing interactions is more ambiguous. There is an absence of objective or sufficiently quantifiable language with which to determine or assess what constitutes acceptable minimum force in a given situation. Interpretation of the term "minimum" is inherently subjective; any incident where risk is evident will inevitably be perceived and responded to differently by individual officers. An assessment of minimum force will depend upon a range of variables, each of which are subject to individual interpretations within particular situational, jurisdictional, organisational and operational contexts. Despite a robust body of research examining police decision-making (such as, Bolger 2015; Miller 2015; Terrill and Paoline 2013; White 2002), there is no algorithm or objective model through which to determine a required policing response or the appropriate level of force to be deployed in any conceivable circumstance.

In practical terms, the operationalisation of minimum force relies upon police discretion, sometimes exercised alone and, often, in situations that are unstable, unpredictable and evolving rapidly (Bronitt and Stenning 2011; Klockars 1985; Mastrofski 2004; Nowacki 2015). A core aspect of any discretionary decision to use force is the choice to deploy one or more of a range of verbal and physical responses. The decision will not only reflect the nature and perceived seriousness of the incident, relevant operational guidelines and individual officer characteristics, it will also be determined by the equipment that is available and to hand. Options may include verbal commands, the use of restraints (such as handcuffs), physical containment, and/or the deployment of various agents designed to incapacitate, such as CS gas, batons, conducted energy devices or firearms. It is self-evident that an officer with limited equipment will be able to draw from a more limited set of discretionary options when compared with an officer in possession of a comprehensive set of offensive and defensive resources.

Perceived legitimacy is a pre-requisite for effective policing (Tyler 2006; Tyler and Wakslak 2004). Legitimacy, as viewed by the community, can be engendered by and manifested through a range of contexts, such as compliance, effectiveness, and procedural justice (see, for example, Bradford and Jackson 2016; Huq et al. 2017; Tyler and Jackson 2014). A key element of police legitimacy is community acceptance that officers use force appropriately and in accordance with public expectations—both of which are embodied within the doctrine of minimum force. When the role played by discretion in any police decision to use force is combined with potentially immediate and lethal use of firearms, the specific risk of harm to individuals intersects with procedural justice and wider notions of legitimacy (Bradford et al. 2017).

Despite the consensus underpinning the concept of minimum force, the use of force by police is a contentious and much discussed topic (see, for example, Bradford and Jackson 2016; Kuhns et al. 2010; Squires and Kennison 2010; Waddington 2007; Waddington and Wright 2010). As the ultimate expression of police power, incidents culminating in the fatal police shooting of civilians garner varying degrees of attention, both with respect to formal investigative provisions under the auspices of the relevant jurisdictional oversight bodies (e.g. criminal, civil or coronial court processes), and through media and other public scrutiny. Individual police shooting incidents may generate national and even global interest. Prominent examples include the June 2017 murder of Justine Damond by police officer Mohammed Noor, in Minneapolis (BBC 2019; Walker 2018), and the fatal shooting in 2005 of Jean Charles de Menezes by specialist armed officers from London's Metropolitan Police (McCulloch and Sentas 2006; Walker 2018). There is generally less attention given to the overall quantum of police shootings (fatal or not) and other expressions of force, both within and between jurisdictions. This is regrettable, because this broader picture is revealing about police use of force, and how minimum force is implemented. The facility for police officers to use force (up to and including lethal force) and the doctrine of minimum force are both embedded within operational policing. But to what extent is the broad acceptance of the routine arming of police officers compatible with the universal expectation of minimum-force policing?

5.3 Study Context and Rationale

That police should and must be armed with powerful and visible weaponry is a view that is entrenched across multiple jurisdictions but which finds its ultimate expression in American policing (see Chap. 3). Armed police and other law enforcement officers are ubiquitous, firearms are worn prominently and drawn readily. Fatal shootings of civilians are far from uncommon. Approximately one in every 1000 black American men will be killed by a police officer. For men between 25 and 29 years old, across all races, being killed by a police officer is the sixth most likely cause of death in America (Edwards et al. 2019). These figures sit in stark contrast to the doctrine of minimum force.

The United States is not an exemplar of minimum force policing, and it is far from typical. Despite its status as the richest and most influential liberal democracy, in terms of policing the United States is an outlier. This reflects a complex range of factors, but particularly the widespread availability of firearms in the community (Zimring 2017). The United States is a key focus of research and media discourse regarding the police use of force (Gerber and Jackson 2017; Paoline et al. 2018). We acknowledge the importance of American scholarly inquiry into police use of force. The global reach of American media also means that American policing attitudes and methods, as transmitted through popular culture, can exert a profound influence on public perceptions and expectations in other jurisdictions (see Chap. 7). However, to increase the external and ecological validity of our study, we have decided not to include an American jurisdiction. Put simply, policing is one context in which American exceptionalism is indisputable, and this makes any attempt at comparative study problematic (see Chap. 1).

Existing research has typically examined the police use of force in relation to individual events; situational, organisational and other factors influencing decision-making processes; or within specific jurisdictions, whether at local or national level. Comparative jurisdictional approaches are more limited. Knutsson and Strype (2003) and Hendy (2014) both examined police officer attitudes to the carriage and use of firearms in Norway (routinely unarmed) and Sweden (routinely armed). Osse and Cano (2017) collected data from 11 countries and compared the number of deaths caused by police use of firearms with national homicide rates (although in only one of the 11 jurisdictions were police not routinely armed). More recently, Hendy (2019) analysed police conflict resolution in New Zealand (routinely unarmed) and South Australia (routinely armed). With a focus on gun control, Sarre (2019) compared gun violence, associated operational and legislative responses, and their effects, in Australia and the United States.

Our current study follows a four-jurisdiction comparative model, and examines key data from: Manchester, England/Wales; Toronto, Canada; Auckland, New Zealand; and Brisbane, Australia. The four locations which form the basis of our study are broadly comparable. English is the official language and the dominant (but not the only) community language, and British political and legal traditions are common-place. Government is democratic and generally stable, with relatively prosperous underpinning capitalist economies. Each has a notable colonial history, rooted in British Imperialism, and associated traditions of discrimination and socio-economic disadvantage experienced by particular ethnic/racial groups. The four locations are all officially secular, all share a traditional but fading Christian influence, and now have a diverse multi-culture of faith traditions and organisations. Recent decades have seen the predominant Anglo-centric patriarchal structures challenged, with varying success, by a drive towards greater equality and diversity. Media is generally open and uncensored, social media is ubiquitous, and the right to freedom of expression is a core expectation. Criminal justice has a "tough on crime" focus, and attitudes have generally become more punitive over recent years, but with limited beneficial effects for offenders, victims of crime or the wider community. With respect to the cities, each is a prominent regional centre, but not a national capital.

There are, of course, differences. These include climate, geography, population size and origins, Indigenous heritage and cultural traditions. It is also true that crime data are defined and measured variably, and policing policies are set at different levels of government: all of which need to be factored into any comparison. We acknowledge that these external variables exist. Where possible, and where data allows, we have adjusted for these variables in our analysis. Some variables, especially related to culture and local custom, are difficult to quantify but given the wider homogeneity of the chosen locations, we believe that a comparative study remains valid.

The key difference, for the purposes of this study, is that each country varies in the extent to which police are routinely armed. In England and Wales, and New Zealand, operational police *do not* routinely carry firearms. In Australia and Canada, operational police *do* routinely carry firearms. Given their many similarities, these jurisdictions are ideal locations to undertake an empirical examination of different applications of the use of force by police.

The focus, we emphasise, is on the routine carriage of firearms by operational police officers on regular duty. All four jurisdictions have the capacity to deploy specialist armed response teams if necessary. Such teams are highly trained, and a decision to deploy follows clear protocols within a chain of command. The use of force by such specialist units is qualitatively different from the discretionary, individual and on-the-spot decisions required by regular patrol officers responding immediately to many and varied situations.

Before moving on to set out the research design, we acknowledge the limitations of framing any analysis within a binary 'routinely armed/routinely unarmed' perspective. The operationalisation of minimum force and the effects on safety are determined by more than the routine presence or absence of a firearm. A complex set of drivers underpin and determine specific and general operational responses. These include, but are not limited to, procedural, cultural, situational, political, demographic, and individual officer characteristics. Accepting these limitations, at a macro level, meaningful comparisons can be made to test assumptions and to inform understanding of the wider effects of policing with or without the routine presence of firearms. To discern a direct causal relationship between the routine presence or absence of a police firearm and various indictors of risk and community safety is complex, and sits outside of the scope of our current analysis. Rather, we seek to establish the quantum of risk associated with routinely armed or unarmed police, and to examine correlations between key measures of safety and the presence or absence of firearms. Our purpose is to begin the development of an empirically informed understanding of the effect of routinely armed and routinely unarmed police on the application of the doctrine of minimum force, an evidence-based understanding which is not driven by assumptions and rhetoric.

We do not claim to have established all of the answers; our focus is to start to ask the right questions.

5.4 The Operationalisation of Minimum Force

There is no universal definition of the use of force or how minimum force is operationalised. The International Association of Chiefs of Police (2001) offers the following description: "[the] amount of effort required by police to compel compliance by an unwilling subject." How this is interpreted is subjective and almost impossible to quantify. Across the four locations that we have examined, similar vagaries are evident within policing policy and practices. It is necessary, then, to briefly summarise the approaches to operationalising minimum force in each location.

5.4.1 England and Wales

Greater Manchester Police is one of the 43 regional police forces in England/Wales (Police.UK 2020). All are governed by separate leadership hierarchies but operate under the auspices of national legislation, such as the *Police Act*, 2002. With respect to the use of force by police, section 3 of the Criminal*Law Act* 1967, states: "A person may use such force as is reasonable in the circumstances in the prevention of crime, or in effecting or assisting in the lawful arrest of offenders or suspected offenders or of persons unlawfully at large." These expectations are conceptually clear but there is little information to help with an objective assessment of what constitutes proportionate or reasonable behaviour in any given circumstance. The 2008 *Criminal Justice and Immigration Act* added a further layer of complication by specifying that the legal interpretation of "reasonable" includes the genuine belief of the person using the force—whether or not that belief was subsequently determined to be objectively correct.[3] Discretion, then, underpins the use of force by police officers in England and Wales, including in Manchester (TNS-BMRB 2015; IPCC 2016). But one option that is not available to all officers is the use of a firearm.

---

[3]Under Scottish law, specific guidance is provided on the use of firearms—as the most serious use of force option: "a police officer is not entitled to discharge a firearm against a person unless the officer has reasonable grounds for believing that the person is committing, or about to commit, an action likely to endanger the life or cause serious injury to the officer or any other person, and there is no other way to prevent the danger" (College of Policing 2018).

5.4.2 Canada

In November 2000, the Canadian Association of Chiefs of Police (CACP) issued The National Use of Force Framework (CACP 2000). The Framework embodies a wheel of "use of force" options, to counter any perception that the choice of force should progress in a linear manner. The Framework is not intended to dictate operational policy, to prescribe specific responses to situations, or to justify an officer's use of force (CACP 2000, p. 3). The first three of six prescribed principles within the Framework are: (1) *The primary responsibility of a peace officer is to preserve and protect life; (2) The primary objective of any use of force is to ensure public safety; (3) Police officer safety is essential to public safety.*

The city of Toronto is located in the province of Ontario. The Toronto Police Service (TPS) operates under the Ontario Use of Force Model, which was developed from the National Framework. The model requires officers to undertake a proactive and continual assessment, and to determine the most reasonable response given the circumstances. In 2014, the TPS was urged to revise its Use of Force Procedure to minimise the use of lethal force, to emphasise its use as a last resort in crisis situations, and to prioritise the preservation of life (Lacobucci 2014: 25). The 2014 report emphasised a target of "zero deaths when police interact with a member of the public" (p. 8). A common theme across more recent Canadian investigations of 'use of force' mechanisms is the desire for a greater emphasis upon de-escalation, but there is limited guidance on how this should be achieved (Dube 2016; McNeilly 2017).

5.4.3 New Zealand

New Zealand has a single, national police organisation. The jurisdiction of New Zealand Police includes the city of Auckland, which is the nation's largest city (though not its capital). In New Zealand, the use of force by police is regulated by the *Crimes Act*, 1961, which permits "such force as may be necessary to overcome any force used." Again, objective assessment is vague but, under section 62, officers are criminally liable for demonstrable use of excessive force. The use of force, and of firearms in particular, is governed by the Police General Instructions. The overriding requirement is that "minimum force must be applied to effect the purpose. Where practical Police should not use a firearm unless it can be done without endangering other persons" (FO61—Use of Firearms by Police: NZ Police 2019). In addition, the principle of minimum personal carriage and minimum visibility of firearms and related equipment must be applied at all times (F060—Carrying of Firearms by Police). The permissible circumstances in which a police officer may use a firearm is set out more specifically. These include defending themselves or others if they fear death or grievous bodily harm (*Crimes Act* 1961, s.48); arresting an offender if they reasonably believe the offender poses a threat of death or grievous bodily harm (s.39); preventing the escape of an offender who they reasonably believe poses a threat of death or grievous bodily harm (s.40) and who tries to escape; and/or, where possible, the officer has called upon the offender to surrender. A summary of these provisions is printed on the inside cover of Police issue notebooks. While there is some clarity regarding the general circumstances in which a firearm could be used, there remains no objective guidance to assist with a decision to deploy, point or fire. Discretion again prevails.

5.4.4   Australia

Under Australia's Federal system, states and territories are empowered to establish and operate their policing functions autonomously. Brisbane is located in the state of Queensland and, like the rest of the state, is policed by the Queensland Police Service (QPS). The current Queensland Police Operational Procedures Manual (OPM) (QPS 2019: 14.3), states that police officers must "only use the minimum amount of force necessary to safely resolve an incident." All "use of force" applications must be: (i) authorised; (ii) justified; (iii) reasonable/proportionate/appropriate; (iv) legally defensible; and (v) tactically sound and effective. What is missing from the OPM is any objective guide to what is reasonable, proportionate or appropriate in any given context. Discretion remains the primary variable within the model.

Two key themes emerge from this overview of the operationalisation of the use of force across the four locations. First, there is broad consistency with respect to the philosophy and expectation of minimum force. Second, there is a consistent absence of objective clarity within operational policies and processes about decisions to use force. In each jurisdiction, a spectrum of permissible types of force is available, ranging from implied force which comes with the mere presence of an officer, through to lethal force. The words minimum, reasonable and proportionate are used repeatedly, both in legislation and in operational procedures, but each lacks a clear contextual definition and each is inherently subjective in interpretation and application. All four jurisdictions place considerable significance on the expectation and capacity of officers to apply their discretion appropriately and effectively, and to demonstrate reasonableness and proportionality in exercising the minimum force necessary.

Given the similar expectations of the use of force across the four jurisdictions, and the similar reliance on individual officer discretion, the significance of the routine presence or absence of a firearm is amplified. The lack of consensus about how and when to deploy force elevates the importance of the options available to individual officers. Within a continuum of discretionary responses, some jurisdictions permit the on-the-spot selection of lethal force. Of course, individual incidents and situations will differ and responses cannot and should not necessarily be subject to generalisation. However, across comparative jurisdictions, it is appropriate to examine the collective effects of the routine presence of a firearm. At the very least, the oft-repeated assertion that arming police increases safety should be tested. Does ready access by a police officer to a firearm affect the operationalisation of the doctrine of minimum force? And does the routine arming of police make the community safer, or the police themselves safer?

5.5 Research Method

5.5.1 Procedure

Our study has undertaken a comparative analysis of key measures in relation to the use of force by police across the four jurisdictions, examining data at both a national and a city level.

All data has been extracted from publicly available sources for each jurisdiction. Where possible, government, police and other official statistics have been used. In places, gaps have been filled with reference to legal sources, media and other research articles. All data sources are acknowledged within notes for each Table and Figure in Chap. 6.

5.5.2 Analysis

Where possible, data has been analysed at both national and city level. Rather than taking a single year snapshot, data is examined across multiple years; temporal ranges differ according to each analysis and depending on the availability of sufficiently comparable data. This longitudinal focus mitigates the potential effect of minor fluctuations and isolated incidents, such as a terror event or single mass murder upon homicide levels in a given year. Over extended periods of time, if the routine presence and imminent threat of an armed police intervention does indeed correlate with improved levels of community and officer safety, this should be evident within the data.

In Chap. 6 we first set out key descriptive data regarding the relative populations and sworn police numbers in each location; both are used as explanatory variables across the analysis. To provide an indication of comparative and differential levels of risk and to inform discussion of the findings, we then analyse key crime indicators—starting with homicide. As the intentional and unlawful killing of another person, homicide is the most objectively and consistently recorded category of violent crime. It is also the least likely of all offences to be unreported and undetected (Mouzos 2003). The United Nations Office on Drugs and Crime (UNODC 2014: 9) positions homicides as "a reasonable proxy for violent crime, as well as a robust indicator of levels of security within States." Homicides committed using a firearm can, as noted by Osse and Caro (2017: 634), be regarded as "a parallel phenomenon to deaths caused by police use of firearms." Logically, if jurisdictions with routinely armed police are safer, they will record a lower level of homicides. We test this hypothesis by examining homicide numbers (in total, and by weapon type). We also analyse data in relation to robbery, sexual offences, and violence against the person, as well as fatal police shootings of civilians to explore the extent to which the routine presence of a police firearm correlates with community safety. We then examine data in relation to use of force measures and police officer safety: non-accidental police fatalities while on duty; police shootings of civilians; firearm discharge incidents; and recorded use of conducted energy devices (CEDs), to explore whether routinely arming police officers correlates with higher levels of police safety. We have included data on police officers who discharge a firearm, even if no injury results. We have done so because the only valid reason for police to discharge a firearm is a situation in which an officer or another person is under immediate threat of serious harm. The data used specifically excludes accidental discharges, discharges for animal destruction, and the use of firearms during police training and tyre deflations. Thus, it is reasonable to regard police discharge of firearms as a proxy measure of police being in situations of risk or personal danger. The same rationale applies to the use of CEDs.

Findings are set out as absolute figures, and as relative rates by population or sworn police numbers. To further interrogate the numerical differences between jurisdictions and to determine the presence and extent of any statistically significant findings, where sufficient data is available and where relevant, the results from cross-tabulations and negative binomial regression analyses are also documented. Cross-tabulation and regression analyses were undertaken using either SPSS or R-Studio. For each jurisdictional regression analysis, the most notable numerical outlier is assigned as the reference point (constant/intercept) with the other three jurisdictions assigned as co-variates.

5.5.3 Limitations

All of the data examined has been derived from publicly available sources and has not been validated. Comparable data is not available for all jurisdictions for each variable examined. Where necessary, analysis has been limited to a sub-set of juris-dictions. We acknowledge that police use of force is not limited to the use of weapons. Police actions may lead to civilian deaths and injury in other ways, such as excessive restraint, underlying medical issues exacerbated by police interventions, and inade-quate medical attention following interactions with police. These circumstances are more difficult to isolate and are not included in our analysis.

We acknowledge that causal linkages cannot be discerned from the method that has been adopted. However, by identifying notable correlations, valid comparative measures and relevant tests of significance between variables for each location, we are able to highlight key indicators of difference. We present the analysis is a manner that is pragmatic and accessible, and which reflects the purpose of this book. In particular, the use of descriptive analyses and discussion is intentional, and the more complex statistical methods support rather than drive the analysis. The findings set out are not necessarily generalisable, but they are intended to drive discussion, and to challenge generally unquantified assertions of the common-sense need for routinely armed police. In our analysis of the research findings, we note where further examination of the use of force by police is needed, alongside more focused consideration of the operational, philosophical and conceptual principles within which the doctrine of minimum force is applied. Our findings are not intended to be definitive—our purpose is to inform debate and to highlight the need for evidence-based discussion of the routine use of firearms by police officers.

5.6   Chapter Conclusion

In this chapter we have set out the need for an evidence base from which to examine the effects on safety of the routine arming of police officers. Our research rationale and approach are documented, along with acknowledgment of key limitations.

In Chap. 6, we build upon the historical, theoretical and conceptual discussions of the first half of this book to present the findings of our comparative examination of the correlation between community safety, police officer safety, and the routine arming of police officers. We set out our evidence-based assessment of the doctrine of minimum force and of the armed tradition, by exploring key measures of community and police officer safety within jurisdictions where police are either routinely armed or routinely unarmed. We examine whether the principle of minimum force is merely an aphorism, a rhetorical position which is vulnerable to challenge, or whether the efficacy of minimum force policing, for both the community and police themselves, can be demonstrated with tested evidence.

References

Anderson, D. (2017). *Attacks in London and Manchester, March–June 2017. Independent assessment of MI5 and police internal reviews.* London: Brick Court Chambers.
BBC. (2019). Justine Damond: US policeman jailed for Australian's murder. *BBC News Online.* Accessed 9 Dec. 2019.
Bolger, P. C. (2015). Just following orders: A meta-analysis of the correlates of American police officer use of force decisions. *American Journal of Criminal Justice, 40*(3), 466–492.
Bradford, B., & Jackson, J. (2016). Enabling and constraining police power: On the moral regulation of policing. In Jacobs, J. & Jackson, J. (Eds.), *Routledge handbook of criminal justice ethics.* Oxon: Routledge.
Bradford, B., Milani, J., & Jackson, J. (2017). Identity, legitimacy and "making sense" of police use of force. *Policing: An International Journal, 40*(3):614–627.
Bronitt, S., & Stenning, P. (2011). Understanding discretion in modern policing. *Criminal Law Journal, 35,* 319–332.
Bush, M. (2019). Police to pilot Armed Response Teams. [media release] New Zealand Police, 18 Oct. Available from: https://www.police.govt.nz/news/release/police-pilot-armed-response-teams.

CACP. (2000). *A national use of force framework* [online]. Available from: https://www.cacp.ca/cacp-use-of-force-advisory-committee-activities.html?asst_id=199. Accessed 25 Nov 2019.

College of Policing. (2018). *Armed policing: Legal framework* [online]. Available from https://www.app.college.police.uk/app-content/armed-policing/legal-framework/#use-of-force-and-firearms. Accessed 25 Nov 2019.

Crawford, A. (2017). 'Reassurance policing: Feeling is believing. In Henry, A. & Smith, D. J. (Eds.), *Transformations of policing*. Oxon: Routledge.

Dodd, V. (2017). Majority of police officers are prepared to carry guns, survey finds. *The Guardian*, 23 Sept. Accessed 30 Sept 2019.

Dodd, V. (2018). UK police chiefs discuss officers routinely carrying guns. *The Guardian*, 17 May. Accessed 15 Oct 2019.

Dube, P. (2016). *A matter of life and death*. Ontario: Ombudsman of Ontario.

Edwards, F., Lee, H., & Esposito, M. (2019). Risk of being killed by police use of force in the United States by age, race–ethnicity, and sex. *Proceedings of the National Academy of Sciences, 116*(34), 16793–16798.

Eustachewich, L. (2018). Knife attacks and murders spike in the UK. *New York Post*, 19 Jul. Accessed 25 Feb 2019.

Farmer, C., & Evans, R. (2019). Primed and ready: Does arming police increase safety? Preliminary findings. *Violence & Gender* [online first]. https://doi.org/10.1089/vio.2019.0020.

Fielding, N., & Innes, M. (2006). Reassurance policing, community policing and measuring police performance. *Policing and Society, 16*(2), 127–145.

Fleming, J. (2005). 'Working Together': Neighbourhood Watch, reassurance policing and the potential of partnerships. *Trends & Issues in Crime and Criminal Justice*, No. 303, Sept.

Gerber, M. M., & Jackson, J. (2017). Justifying violence: Legitimacy, ideology and public support for police use of force. *Psychology, Crime & Law, 23*(1), 79–95.

Hendy, R. (2014). Routinely armed and unarmed police: What can the Scandinavian experience teach us? *Policing, 8*(2), 183–192.

Hendy, R. (2019). Procedural conflict and conflict resolution: A cross-national study of police officers from New Zealand and South Australia. Ph.D. Thesis. University of Cambridge.

Huq, A., Jackson, J., & Trinkner, R. (2017). Legitimating practices: Revisiting the predicates of police legitimacy. *British Journal of Criminology, 57*(5), 1101–1122.

Iacobucci, F. (2014). *Police encounters with people in crisis: Independent Review of the Toronto Police Service* [online]. Available from: https://www.torontopolice.on.ca/publications/files/reports/police_encounters_with_people_in_crisis_2014.pdf. Accessed 25 Nov 2019.

Independent Police Complaints Commission (IPCC). (2016). *Police use of force*. Available from: https://www.policeconduct.gov.uk/sites/default/files/Documents/research-learning/IPCC_Use_Of_Force_Report.pdf. Accessed 19 Feb 2020.

International Association of the Chiefs of Police. (2001). *Police use of force in America*, Alexandria, Virginia. Available from: https://www.theiacp.org/sites/default/files/2018-08/2001useofforce.pdf. Accessed 30 Nov 2019.

Klockars, C. B. (1985). *The idea of police*. Beverly Hills: Sage Publications.

Knutsson, J., & Strype, J. (2003). Police use of firearms in Norway and Sweden: The significance of gun availability. *Policing & Society, 13*(4), 429–439.

Kuhns, J. B., Knutsson, J., & Bayley, D. H. (2010). *Police use of force: A global perspective*. Santa Barbara, Calif.: Praeger.

Long, T. (2016). *Lethal force*. London: Ebury Press.

Mastrofski, D. (2004). Controlling street-level police discretion. *American Academy of Political and Social Science, 593*(1), 100–118.

McCulloch, J., & Sentas, V. (2006). The killing of Jean Charles de Menezes. *Social Justice, 33*(4), 92–106.

McNeilly, G. (2017). *Police interactions with people in crisis and use of force*. Toronto: Office of the Independent Police Review Director.

Menon, P. (2019). New Zealand plans armed police patrols after Christchurch massacre. *Reuters Online*, 18 October. Available from: https://www.reuters.com/article/us-newzealand-shooting-security/new-zealand-plans-armed-police-patrols-after-christchurch-massacre-idUSKBN1W X00D. Accessed 30 Nov 2019.

Miller, L. (2015). Why cops kill: The psychology of police deadly force encounters. *Aggression and Violent Behaviour, 22* (May–June), 97–111.

Mouzos, J. (2003). Australian homicide rates: A comparison of three data sources. *Trends & Issues in Crime and Criminal Justice, 261* (July). Australian Institute of Criminology.

Nowacki, J. S. (2015). Organizational-level police discretion: An application for police use of lethal force. *Crime & Delinquency, 61*(5), 643–668.

NZ Police. (2019). *Use of firearms by police* [online]. Available from: https://www.police.govt.nz/news/release/3376. Accessed 30 Nov 2019.

Osse, A., & Cano, I. (2017). Police deadly use of firearms: An international comparison. *The International Journal of Human Rights, 21*(5), 629–649.

Paoline, E. A., Gau, J. M., & Terrill, W. (2018). Race and the police use of force encounter in the United States. *British Journal of Criminology, 58*(1), 54–74.

Police.UK. (2020). *Contact the police*. Retrieved from: https://www.police.uk/forces/.

QPS. (2019). *Operational skills and practices*. Queensland Police Service. Available from: https://www.police.qld.gov.au/sites/default/files/2019-10/OPM%20-%20Chapter%2014%20-%20O perational%20Skills%20and%20Practices.pdf. Accessed 25 Nov 2019.

Robinson, M. (2019). England's knife crime epidemic sees 54% rise in young stabbing injuries in 5 years. *CNN International*, 9 February. Available from: https://edition.cnn.com/2019/02/09/uk/knife-crime-violence-stabbings-hospital-admissions-gbr-intl/index.html. Accessed 24 Feb 2019.

Sarre, R. (2019). Gun control: An Australian perspective. In Carlson, J., Goss, K., & Shapira, H. (Eds.), *Gun Studies: Interdisciplinary approaches to politics, policy and practice*. Oxon: Routledge.

Squires, P., & Kennison, P. (2010). *Shooting to kill? Policing, firearms and armed response*. Chichester: Wiley-Blackwell.

Terrill, W., & Paoline, E. A. (2013). Less lethal force policy and police officer perceptions: A multi-site examination. *Criminal Justice and Behaviour, 40*(10), 1109–1130.

TNS-BMRB. (2015). *Police use of force*. Available from: https://www.policeconduct.gov.uk/sites/default/files/Documents/research-learning/BMRB_use_of_force_report.pdf. Accessed 19 Feb 2020.

Tyler, T. R. (2006). *Why people obey the law*. Princeton, NJ: Princeton University Press.

Tyler, T. R., & Jackson, J. (2014). Popular legitimacy and the exercise of legal authority: Motivating compliance, cooperation, and engagement. *Psychology, Public Policy, and Law, 20*(1), 78–95.

Tyler, T. R., & Wakslak, C. J. (2004). Profiling and police legitimacy: Procedural justice, attributions of motive, and acceptance of police authority. *Criminology, 42*(2), 253–281.

University of Sydney. (2019). *GunPolicy.org* [online]. University of Sydney. Available from: https://www.gunpolicy.org/about. Accessed 30 Nov 2019.

UNODC. (2014). *Global study on homicide*. Vienna: UNODC.

Waddington, P. A. J. (2007). Use of force. *Policing: A Journal of Policy and Practice,1*(3), 249–251.

Waddington, P. A. J., & Wright, M. (2010). Police use of guns in unarmed countries: The United Kingdom. In Kuhns, J. B., & Knutsson, J. (Eds.), *Police use of force: A global perspective*. Santa Barbara, Calif.: Praeger.

Walker, D. (2018). *Fatal force: A conversation with journalists who cover deadly, highly-publicized police shootings* (Master's thesis). Available from: https://scholarcommons.sc.edu/etd/4755. Accessed 30 Nov 2019.

White, M. D. (2002). Identifying situational predictors of police shootings using multivariate analysis. *Policing: An International Journal of Police Strategies & Management, 25*(4), 726–751.

Zimring, F. E. (2017). *When police kill*. Cambridge, Mass: Harvard University Press.

Chapter 6
'The Law of the Instrument': Examining the Nexus Between Safety and the Routine Arming of Police Officers

Abstract This chapter builds on the historical, theoretical and conceptual discussions of previous chapters, and presents the findings of our comparative examination of community safety, police officer safety, and the routine arming of police officers. We explore how safety, a complex construct, can be usefully measured, and then compare in detail the four chosen jurisdictions. Using publicly available data, published documents and media sources, we analyse patterns of crime, behaviour and risk, and explore the relationship between the routine arming of police officers, community and police officer safety. Precise causal relationships are difficult to establish with certainty. Our analysis is framed within a "positive effect" construct. The armed tradition of policing is underpinned by the assertion that the routine arming of police enables and ensures both community and police officer safety (see Chap. 4). If this assertion is correct, then in jurisdictions where police officers are routinely armed, the occurrence and rates of key categories of crime will be lower than in jurisdictions whose police are deployed without routinely carrying firearms, as will key measures of police officer safety. We also explore the idea of the "law of the instrument": the proposition that the availability of a particular response increases the likelihood that it will be used, even in situations where other solutions are more appropriate. This principle would predict that routinely armed police are more likely to use firearms in situations where such use is not absolutely essential, even though all four jurisdictions have clear expectations of minimum-force policing (see Chap. 3). We conclude that the claimed benefits of the armed tradition of policing—a safer community protected by safer police officers—are not supported by the evidence. There is also some evidence to support the law of the instrument: routinely armed police are more likely to use firearms, despite operating under the same minimum-force doctrine as their unarmed colleagues.

6.1 Introduction

Over the past thirty years across Western jurisdictions, police have steadily become more militarised (see Chap. 4). Mummolo (2018: 9181) describes the structural, tactical, cultural and equipment changes that are embodied within and by police militarisation. A fundamental aspect is the routine carriage of firearms, the transition to more powerful firearms, and making such weapons more numerous and more visible. This trend is especially evident in the United States (Delehanty et al. 2017) but also observable in other jurisdictions, including Australia (Funnell 2019; Goldsworthy 2014). In the United States, under the 1033 Program, the Department of Defence distributes surplus military equipment to more than 8600 law enforcement agencies across the nation (Delehanty et al. 2017). The effect of the program was clear in the police response to rioting in Ferguson, Missouri in 2014. Officers arrived in an armoured vehicle, dressed in military fatigues with assault rifles in hand (Funnell 2019). Police in Australia are also engaging with more militarised equipment. Goldsworthy (2014) reports the use, by the Queensland Police Service, of military-style drones, their purchase of military assault rifles for general duty police officers, and the use, by Western Australia Police, of armoured vehicles. He attributes the drive towards more militarised police to an unsubstantiated panic over the fear of crime, and of terrorism in particular, for which more powerful policing capabilities are perceived to be an essential response (Goldsworthy, quoted in Funnell 2019).

The effects of such police militarisation are not inherently beneficial. Mummolo (2018) finds no demonstrable benefits for community safety (by way, for example, of a reduction in key categories of crime) and concluded that police militarisation may not serve the needs or interests of the community. In an examination of the link between equipment transfers under the 1033 Program and fatalities from officer-involved shootings in four US states, Delehanty et al. (2017) identifies a strong correlation. Our purpose here is not to provide a foundation from which to examine the role or effects of police militarisation per se. The relevance, as Delehanty et al. (2017) established, is that access to militarised equipment increases the likelihood of more violent outcomes. This embodies the concept of the "law of the instrument", as formulated by Abraham Kaplan: "Give a small boy a hammer, and he will find that everything he encounters needs pounding" (Kaplan 1964: 28). In other words, the availability of a particular response increases the likelihood that it will be used, even in situations where other solutions may be objectively more appropriate.[1] It is this potential connection that informs and supports the framing of our study.

According to Kraska (2007: 3) "[e]valuating police militarization is a credible and important endeavour, and it can be accomplished through empirical evidence and rigorous scholarship." The steady militarisation of policing continues to generate scrutiny and focused research. Yet, despite the broadly accepted norm of routinely armed police officers, we have been unable to locate any published material which applies an evidence-base, rather than opinion or perception, to support assertions of a beneficial safety effect for officers themselves or the community.

---

[1]The 'law of the instrument' and associated reference to a boy and hammer is believed to be derived from a 19th Century London periodical. Its first use in an academic context is attributed to Philosophy Professor Abraham Kaplan in a speech to the American Educational Research Association, in February 1962 (Horowitz 1962: 637). The following quote appears in a subsequent publication: "I call it *the law of the instrument,* and it may be formulated as follows: Give a small boy a hammer, and he will find that everything he encounters needs pounding" (Kaplan 1964: 28).

Our research design is framed within a "positive effect" construct. By this, we interpret the rhetoric used within the armed tradition as amounting to a positive claim: that the routine arming of police enables and ensures both community and police officer safety. It is reasonable to expect, if this truth-claim has merit, that in jurisdictions where police officers are routinely armed, the occurrence and rates of key categories of crime will be lower than in jurisdictions whose police are deployed without routinely carrying firearms. Similarly, routinely armed jurisdictions will exhibit better outcomes in terms of key measures of police officer safety.

Chapter 5 sets out the rationale for the study, explains our choice of jurisdictions, details the research approach, and acknowledges key limitations. Of particular methodological importance is the recognition that causal linkages cannot be discerned from the method that has been adopted. By examining a range of comparative measures between variables for each location, we highlight key correlations and indicators of difference. The findings are intended to drive discussion by challenging the generally unquantified assertions of the "common-sense" need for routinely armed police. We also draw out where further analysis of the use of force by police is needed, alongside more focused consideration of the operational, philosophical and conceptual principles within which the doctrine of minimum force is applied.

The presentation of results starts with descriptive data regarding the relative populations and sworn police officer numbers in each location; both are used as explanatory variables across the analysis. To understand community safety, to provide an indication of comparative levels of "risk" and to inform discussion of the other findings, we analyse and compare key crime indicators, including homicides (in total, and by weapon type), assault, rape and robbery. We then consider data from which to examine police safety: fatal and non-fatal police shootings of civilians; firearm discharge incidents/deployment patterns; recorded use of conducted energy devices (CEDs); and non-accidental deaths of police officers on duty.

Findings are presented at national and/or city level. They are set out as absolute numbers, and as relative rates by population. To examine the extent to which key differences are statistically significant, cross-tabulations and negative binomial regression analyses have been undertaken, using either SPSS or R-Studio.[2]

6.2 Community and Police Safety

The notion of safety is complex and multi-faceted. Being and feeling safe mean different things to different people in different contexts. Individual, group and community sensibilities inform perceptions and expectations of safety, and are as important as any "reality" that may be derived from analysis of empirical data. Gray et al. (2011) offer an expansive theoretically-rich analysis of public insecurities

---

[2]This analysis was supported by Strategic Data Pty Ltd, funded through an internal Deakin University School of Humanities & Social Sciences grant.

regarding crime. They explore the link between the fear and risk of key crime categories and emphasise the need for more effective data driven understanding. However, where the "reality" is either not known or is based upon unsubstantiated presumption, perceptions and associated fears may be misplaced. Police safety is similarly informed by and framed within a range of inter-related factors. For example, police perceptions of the dangers they face will inevitably be reflected in their policing responses. Gibbs (2019) highlights perceptions among US police officers of a "war on cops", arising in part from negative media and public reactions to the policing of high-profile events, such as in Ferguson, Missouri in 2014. In an examination of this rhetoric, White et al. (2019) analyse police deaths on duty (intentional and accidental) and find that, in the United States at least, policing is safer today than fifty years ago. While deaths in the line of duty may have decreased, between 2008 and 2012 the rate of police officer suicides in the US was twice that of intentional killings by other parties (Nanavaty 2015). The cause of an individual suicide cannot necessarily be attributed to policing, but the inter-connectivity between the reality and perception of risk remains.

For the purposes of our study (as set out in Chap. 5), we operationalise community safety in relation to crime-specific data. We have located and compared published data for a range of crime indicators.[3] As such, our analysis of community safety is derived from, and relates to, the extent of reported criminal offending across key crime categories for each of the four jurisdictions. As every scholar of crime and offending is aware, crime data is flawed: problems include the competence and reliability of data gathering organisations, contrasting assumptions about and definitions of various offences, and of course the "dark figure" of unreported/unrecorded offences. Some issues, such as inconsistent definitions across jurisdictions, can be adjusted for. Others, such as the "dark figure" affect all jurisdictions, and presumably to much the same extent. In short, crime data, for all its acknowledged weaknesses, remains a valuable means of comparing jurisdictions. To rework a common metaphor, we are comparing apples with apples, even if the apples might be of poor quality.

We have examined data relating to a number of serious crimes—homicide (overall and by weapon type), robbery, assault and rape—and have examined the fatal shooting of civilians by police officers. The fatal and non-fatal shooting of civilians by police officers is also used as a measure of police safety: such an intervention is regarded as a potential indicator of imminent risk to the officer as well as to the community. We extend our operationalisation of police safety to include firearms discharge incidents (regardless of injury caused) and the use the CEDs, as both provide another indication of situational risk to police officers. Finally, we examine recorded data for non-accidental deaths of police officers while on-duty.

---

[3] Australia's federal system of governance empowers each state/territory to determine their own criminal law provisions. With respect to key crime categories and associated offences, there is minimal definitional difference between the jurisdictions. As Brisbane is located in Queensland, the relevant Queensland legislation has been used in this study.

By conducting a comparative study, our analysis has been limited in places by differential approaches to the recording and/or reporting of data. We have strived to ensure that the categories examined are as objectively and consistently recorded as possible. For example, we have not been able to explore data relating to the number and type of injuries to on duty police officers. Jurisdictions record this data in ways that are notably different, and it is not possible to ensure sufficient comparability. Across our study, we set out relevant definitions and clarify the scope of our analysis.

As discussed earlier, our research design is framed within a "positive effect" construct: that the routine arming of police enables and ensures both community and police officer safety. The expectation is that in the jurisdictions where police officers are routinely armed, the occurrence and rates of key categories of crime will be lower than in jurisdictions whose police are deployed without routinely carrying firearms, as will key measures of police officer safety. This expectation reflects both an inherent protective and a presumed deterrent effect. In relation to crime, the role and effect of deterrence aligns with a rational choice perspective of human behaviour. We recognise that the remit of deterrence is broad. The effects are neither uni-directional nor siloed, but deterrence theories presume that the behaviour of individuals and the community is influenced by the perceived risk of particular consequences (see, for example, Ehrlich 1972; Nagin and Pogarsky 2001; Tonry 2008; von Hirsch et al. 1999). Of relevance to the effect of routinely armed police is the notion of perceptual deterrence, which draws on presumptions of rational decision-making, whereby individuals weigh up the possible benefits of a given act against the probable risks. This cognitive effect is typically framed with respect to the likelihood, celerity and severity of punishment or sanction (Becker 1968; Mann et al. 2016), but can also apply to the risk of more immediate responses, such as the discharge of a police firearm. Perceptual deterrence is not homogeneous: some people are more deterred than others, with the level of deterrence reflecting a range of variables and circumstances (see, for example, Jacobs 2010; Matthews and Agnew 2008; McGrath 2009). However, there is no evidence to suggest that such variations will not be broadly consistent across comparable jurisdictions, hence our examination of data at a national and city level.

6.3 Research Findings: Community and Police Safety

All of the data examined in this chapter has been derived from publicly available sources, primarily government, police and other official statistics. We have not validated any of the data, but it has been extracted from official sources and relates to recorded offences. All data sources are acknowledged within notes for each Table or Figure. Where gaps in official sources makes it necessary, data has been supplemented with information obtained from other research, reports or media coverage. Where possible, analysis has been undertaken across consistent time periods for all jurisdictions. Where data is not available for all years or for all jurisdictions, or where time periods vary, this is made clear within the findings.

6.3.1 Population Data: National and City

Population data is used across the analysis as an explanatory variable, and to increase the comparability of key measures, by enabling data to be presented per 100,000 of population. Figures 6.1 and 6.2 set out the annual national and city population, for each of the jurisdictions, for the period 2007–2017. All four countries and cities show a steady increase in population across the ten-year period. The relative population sizes are clear, with England/Wales the most populous nation and New Zealand the

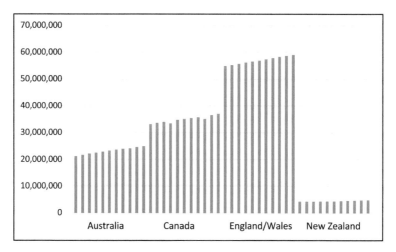

Fig. 6.1 Annual national population: 2007–2017 (All population data sources are set out in note (i))

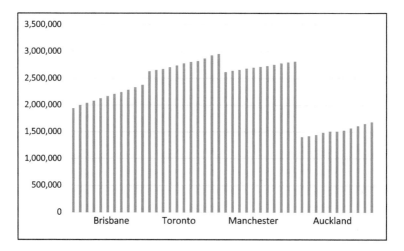

Fig. 6.2 Annual city population: 2007–2017 (All population data sources are set out in note (i))

Table 6.1 Mean population for the period, by jurisdiction: 2007–2017

Jurisdiction (Country)	Mean Population (2007–2017)	Jurisdiction (City)	Mean Population (2007–2017)
England/Wales	56,787,700	Manchester	2,719,000
Canada	34,692,000	Toronto	2,780,000
New Zealand	4,479,000	Auckland	1,512,000
Australia	23,022,000	Brisbane	2,162,000

All population data sources are set out in note (i)

least. For the cities, Toronto and Manchester have broadly similar numbers, with Auckland the least populous. The magnitude of the differences between the most and least populous is less at city than at a national level.

To facilitate the use of relative rates across this chapter, Table 6.1 sets out the mean population for each jurisdiction. This has been calculated by adding up annual population data for each year, 2007–2017, and dividing by the number of years (11). Across our analysis, depending upon the data that is available, different time periods have been examined. Where possible the mean data for the period 2007–2017 is used. Should an alternative calculation be appropriate, this is made clear within the analysis.

6.3.2   Sworn Police Personnel: National and City

Sworn police personnel numbers are also used as an explanatory variable, particularly in relation to measures of police officer safety. These figures relate to operational police officers, and excludes administrative and other support staff. The core data at national level, for the period 2014–2018 are set out in Table 6.2. England/Wales is the only jurisdiction to record a steady decline in police numbers (nearly 4%) over the period examined.

At city level, the available data is more fragmented. Table 6.3 sets out the figures for the period 2010–2018.

Table 6.2 Sworn police personnel numbers (full-time equivalent), at national level: 2014–2018

Year	Australia	Canada	England/Wales	New Zealand
2014	52,211	68,806	127,077	8,818
2015	52,738	68,772	125,574	8,923
2016	53,383	68,859	122,859	8,899
2017	53,857	69,025	121,929	8,834
2018	55,278	68,562	122,395	9,017
MEAN	**53,493**	**68,805**	**123,967**	**8,898**

All sworn police personnel data sources (national and city) are set out in note (ii)

Table 6.3 Sworn police personnel numbers (full-time equivalent), at city level: 2010–2018

Year	Brisbane	Toronto	Manchester	Auckland
2010	2,426	5,636	7,976	717
2011	2,396	5,629	7,656	695
2012	2,475	5,457	7,323	808
2013		5,373	7,069	855
2014		5,335	6,844	829
2015	2,248	5,360	6,484	811
2016	2,247	5,249	6,239	845
2017	2,143		6,237	805
2018		5,000	6,391	804
MEAN	**2,323**	**5,380**	**6,913**	**797**

All sworn police personnel data sources (national and city) are set out in note (ii)

Table 6.4 Sworn police officers per 100,000 population for all jurisdictions

Jurisdiction (Country)	Police per 100,000 population (2014–2018)	Jurisdiction (City)	Police per 100,000 population (2010–2018)
England/Wales	218	Manchester	254
Canada	198	Toronto	194
New Zealand	199	Auckland	53
Australia	232	Brisbane	107

All population and sworn police personnel data sources (national and city) are set out in notes (i) and (ii)

To support comparative analysis across this chapter, we have calculated the number of sworn police officers per 100,000 population at both national and city level. Using the mean populations from Table 6.1, and the mean number of sworn police officers from Tables 6.2 and 6.3, we calculated the number of officers per 100,000 population, set out in Table 6.4.

6.3.3 Key Crime Indicators

To interrogate the relative level of "risk" and attendant community safety in each of our jurisdictions, we have examined patterns and trends in relation to four serious crimes/offence categories: homicide (overall and by weapon type), robbery, violent assault and rape. For each offence type, data is presented at national and city level.

6.3.4 Homicide

As the intentional and unlawful killing of another person, the offence of homicide is more objectively and consistently recorded than other category of violent crime. It is also the least likely of all offences to be unreported and undetected (Mouzos 2003). The United Nations Office on Drugs and Crime (UNODC) positions homicide as "a reasonable proxy for violent crime, as well as a robust indicator of levels of security within States" (UNODC 2014: 9). Homicides committed using a firearm could, as noted by Osse and Caro (2017: 634), be regarded as "a parallel phenomenon to deaths caused by police use of firearms". Logic would suggest that if jurisdictions with routinely armed police are safer, they will record a lower level of homicides.

6.3.4.1 Homicide: Analysis by Country

We first set out key descriptive data for homicide numbers (total and gun-related), at national level (sufficiently comparable data is not available for each city). Relative rates of total homicides, and gun-related homicides, by population, are calculated and compared. To examine the extent to which differences are statistically significant, cross-tabulations and negative binomial regression analyses were undertaken, using either SPSS or R-Studio. For each jurisdictional regression analysis, the most notable numerical outlier was assigned as the reference point (constant or intercept) with the other three jurisdictions assigned as co-variates.

Table 6.5 documents annual homicide numbers, and homicides committed using a firearm, for each of the four countries, for the period 2007–2017.

Table 6.6 collates the annualised data to summarise the total number of homicides for each country over the ten-year period, and the number of gun-related homicides as a percentage of the total.

To ensure a clearer comparison between the countries, Table 6.7 sets out the key variables a s arate per 100,000 people.

The overall homicide rate is highest in Canada, but not by a notable margin when compared with New Zealand. The rates in Australia and England/Wales are similar, with Australia only slightly higher. These findings show that homicide rates are broadly comparable between the countries with no clear pattern evident. As such, they do not support the contention that the routinely armed jurisdictions are safer, when using homicide rates as a measure of the risk of violence.

By contrast, the rate of gun-related homicides in Canada, per 100,000 population, is more than seven times higher than in England/Wales, more than three times higher than in Australia, and two-and-a-half times higher than in New Zealand. The rate in Australia is twice that of England/Wales. Interestingly, the rate in New Zealand is three times that of England/Wales, and marginally higher than in Australia. The number of civilians fatally shot by police shows even greater variance. In Canada the rate, per 100,000 population, is more than 18 times higher than England/Wales, three times higher than Australia, and twice the rate of New Zealand. All other nations

Table 6.5 Homicide numbers by country per year: 2007–2017

Year	Country	Gun Homicide	Total Homicide	Year	Country	Gun Homicide	Total Homicide
2007	England/Wales	58	712	2007	Canada	188	597
2008	England/Wales	53	729	2008	Canada	201	614
2009	England/Wales	39	639	2009	Canada	180	610
2010	England/Wales	41	595	2010	Canada	170	554
2011	England/Wales	60	633	2011	Canada	154	598
2012	England/Wales	40	526	2012	Canada	170	543
2013	England/Wales	29	544	2013	Canada	133	505
2014	England/Wales	29	521	2014	Canada	156	521
2015	England/Wales	21	510	2015	Canada	179	604
2016	England/Wales	26	570	2016	Canada	214	611
2017	England/Wales	32	706	2017	Canada	267	660
2007	New Zealand	5	68	2007	Australia	29	266
2008	New Zealand	7	70	2008	Australia	30	273
2009	New Zealand	14	98	2009	Australia	36	264
2010	New Zealand	8	74	2010	Australia	37	258
2011	New Zealand	7	61	2011	Australia	29	280
2012	New Zealand	6	64	2012	Australia	40	287
2013	New Zealand	13	62	2013	Australia	41	271
2014	New Zealand	7	57	2014	Australia	32	269
2015	New Zealand	14	67	2015	Australia	36	262
2016	New Zealand	11	57	2016	Australia	41	256
2017	New Zealand	12	45	2017	Australia	43	256

All homicide data sources are set out in note (iii)

Table 6.6 Gun homicides as a percentage of total homicides, by country: 2007–2017

Years	Country	Total Homicides	Gun Homicides	Gun Homicides as % of Total (%)
2007–17	England/Wales	6685	428	6.4
2007–17	Canada	6417	2012	31.4
2007–17	New Zealand	723	104	14.4
2007–17	Australia	2942	394	13.4

All homicide data sources are set out in note (iii)

Table 6.7 Relative rates of homicide and gun homicide, by country: 2007–2017

Years	Country	Homicide rate per 100,000 population	Gun Homicide rate per 100,000 population
2007–17	England/Wales	11.77	0.75
2007–17	Canada	18.50	5.80
2007–17	New Zealand	16.14	2.32
2007–17	Australia	12.78	1.71

All homicide and population data sources are set out in notes (i) and (iii)

are notably higher than England/Wales but of interest again is New Zealand, where the rate is approaching twice that of Australia. These findings again show a mixed pattern but, overall, they also fail to demonstrate the presumed community safety benefits of routinely armed police.

Negative binomial regression analyses were run for the core variables: total homicide numbers and gun-related homicides, for each country. Each core variable was modelled as a function of year and country, with population used as an exposure adjustment. The results for homicides are set out in Table 6.8 and gun-related homicides in Table 6.9.

Using Canada as the reference point (intercept), homicide numbers across the period are significantly lower in England/Wales (62%; p-value < 0.001) and Australia (68%; p-value < 0.001). Numbers are also lower in New Zealand, but the difference is less significant (88%; p-value < 0.05).

Table 6.8 Negative binomial regression analysis of total homicide numbers, per 1,000,000 population (Canada as intercept): 2007–2017

	Estimate	Std. Error	RR	Z value	Pr (>|z|)
England/Wales	0.470491	0.044688	0.62	−10.528	< 2e−16***
Australia	0.385012	0.046968	0.68	−8.197	2.46e−16***
New Zealand	0.127298	0.057694	0.88	−2.206	0.0274*

Significance codes (p-value): '***' 0.001 '**' 0.01 '*' 0.05 '.' 0.1 ' ' 1

Table 6.9 Negative binomial regression analysis of total gun-related homicide numbers, per 1,000,000 population (England/Wales as intercept): 2007–2017

	Estimate	Std. Error	RR	Z value	Pr (>|z|)
Australia	0.973414	0.108067	2.65	9.008	<2e−16***
Canada	2.169234	0.094245	8.75	23.017	<2e−16***
New Zealand	1.390929	0.131828	4.02	10.551	<2e−16***

Significance codes (p-value): '***' 0.001 '**' 0.01 '*' 0.05 '.' 0.1 ' ' 1

Table 6.10 Homicide numbers by type: 2009–2016

Country	Gun	Stab	BFT	Other	Total
England/Wales	285	1709	395	2150	4538
Canada	1356	1502	920	768	4546
Australia	292	737	513	605	2147
New Zealand	80	138	174	148	540

All homicide data sources are set out in note (iii)

Table 6.11 Homicide by type, as a percentage of the total number of homicides: 2009–2016

Country	Gun (%)	Stab (%)	BFT (%)	Other (%)
England/Wales	6.28	37.66	8.70	47.38
Canada	29.83	33.04	20.24	16.89
Australia	13.60	34.33	23.89	28.18
New Zealand	14.81	25.56	32.22	27.41

These results demonstrate how much more significant the risk of homicide is in Canada when compared with the other jurisdictions. They confirm that when homicide is used as the measure of violence, there is no discernible benefit to community safety in routinely armed jurisdictions.

The results for gun-related homicides are even more stark, as set out in Table 6.9. Using England/Wales as the reference point (intercept), homicide numbers across the period are significantly higher in Canada (875%; p-value < 0.001), New Zealand (402%; p-value < 0.001) and Australia (265%; p-value < 0.001). Overall, the findings suggest that there is no discernible community safety effect—when gun-related homicide is used as the measure of violence—for those living in routinely armed jurisdictions. That the rate of gun-related homicide is higher in New Zealand than in Australia is an interesting nuance, and merits further analysis of homicide patterns in both countries.

6.3.4.2   Homicide by Type: Analysis by Country

To expand the analysis, we looked at a range of alternative homicide types. This data was only available at a national level, and comparative data could be located for all jurisdictions only for the period 2009–2016. Table 6.10 summarises the total number of homicides by type: gun, stabbing/blade, blunt force trauma (BFT) and "other".[4] Tables 6.11 and 6.12 represent the data as a percentage of the total number of homicides and per 100,000 population.[5] Figure 6.3 provides a visual depiction of the homicides by type per 100,000 population.

---

[4]"Other" includes poisoning, hitting, kicking, asphyxiation, and burning among a range of other homicide methods.

[5]Using the mean population for the period 2007–2017, as set out in Table 6.1.

Table 6.12 Homicide by type per 100,000 population: 2009–2016

Country	Gun	Stab	BFT	Other	Total
England/Wales	0.50	3.01	0.70	3.79	7.99
Canada	3.91	4.33	2.65	2.21	13.10
Australia	1.27	3.20	2.23	2.63	9.33
New Zealand	1.79	3.08	3.88	3.30	12.06

Calculated using mean population data set out in Table 6.1
All population and homicide data sources are set out in notes (i) and (iii)

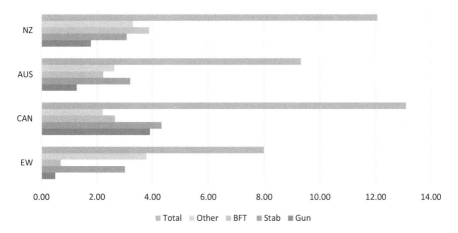

Fig. 6.3 Homicide by type per 100,000 population: 2009–2016

With respect to the cause of homicides across each country, the relative percentages show a general level of consistency, allowing a reasonable margin of error with respect to the precise categorisation for each offence. In addition to the rates of gun-related homicides, the key difference is a notably lower level of BFT-homicide in England/Wales, when compared with the other jurisdictions.

Despite the different time period under analysis (2009–2016, rather than 2007–2017), the overall pattern with respect to the risk of homicide remains consistent. Canada has the highest homicide rate per 100,000 population, followed by New Zealand, Australia and then England/Wales. While the precise figures vary according to the years analysed, the outcome is consistent. Other than the very low level of BFT in England/Wales, no statistically significant differences were identified for stabbing or other homicides. Therefore, using homicide as a measure of community safer, we find no evidence at a national level to indicate that the routinely armed jurisdictions are inherently safer.

Table 6.13 Homicide numbers and rate per 100,000 population for each city: 2013–2017

City	Total Homicides	Homicides per 100,000 population
Manchester	235	8.64
Toronto	313	11.26
Auckland	65	4.3
Brisbane	186	8.6

All population and homicide data sources are set out in notes (i) and (iii)

6.3.4.3   Homicide: Analysis by City

We repeated our analysis at a city level, to ascertain any effect of a more focused perspective. Data was located only for total homicide numbers for the period 2013–2017. There was not sufficient data available to enable a year-by-year comparison or by homicide type. Table 6.13 sets out the aggregated homicide numbers for the period, and rate per 100,000 population.

In common with the national analysis, the rate (and therefore risk) of homicide per 100,000 population was highest in the Canadian city of Toronto. The English and Australian cities of Manchester and Brisbane recorded rates similar to each other, as was the case at a national level. For this analysis, Auckland in New Zealand recorded a notably lower level of homicides per 100,000 than all of the other cities: nearly three times lower than Toronto, and approximately half that of Manchester and Brisbane.

The relative lack of homicides in Auckland is an interesting finding—as the analysis at national level suggests other locations in New Zealand may experience far higher rates, which would merit examination of situational, social and other factors, in a different study. However, once again, for our purposes we can find no evidence to support the presumption that routinely arming police officers increases community safety. Homicide rates are not consistently lower in the cities which deploy routinely armed police.

6.3.5   Other Major Crime Indicators

To further assess levels of risk in relation to key crime indicators, data has been collated and analysed for the offences of assault, rape and robbery. Before setting out our findings, we clarify the precise offences that have been included within each category for each jurisdiction.

Assault

Offence categories are variously recorded and reported within each jurisdiction as common assault, assault causing injury, assault causing bodily harm, or simply as assault. Precise definitions change over time, but consistency of data gathering has been maintained as far as possible. In New Zealand (*Crimes Act* 1961 (NZ)), the offences of common assault, aggravated assault, assault with a weapon are included within the analysis. In England/Wales (*Criminal Justice Act* 1988 (UK); *Offences Against the Person Act* 1861 (UK)), the analysis includes the following non-fatal offences against the person: common assault, actual bodily harm, malicious wounding, and grievous bodily harm. In Canada, assault is defined under Sect. 265 of the *Canadian Criminal Code* and includes assault, assault with a weapon, assault causing bodily harm and aggravated assault. In Australia, at a national level data is collated in relation to assault and violence against the person (for example *Criminal Code* 1899, s. 245 (QLD) defines the key offences). In both Canada and Australia, data has been located in relation to the definitions provided.

Rape

The jurisdictions differ in their definition of rape as an offence, but in all non-consensual sexual activity is outlawed. In New Zealand, rape sits within the statutory offence of sexual violation, under the *Crimes Act* 1961, s.128 (NZ). In England/Wales, the common law offence of rape was codified under Sect. 6.1 of the *Sexual Offences Act* 2003 (UK). In Australia, rape is again defined within each jurisdiction (such as *Criminal Code* 1899, s.349 (QLD). In Canada, Sect. 273 of the *Canadian Criminal Code* 1985 criminalises rape as a form of sexual assault without consent. While the precise categorisations differ slightly, the behaviour that constitutes rape is consistent. It is expected that recorded rape data will reflect comparable behaviours. Rape offences are known to be under-reported, by men and women (see, for example, Allen 2007; Lehner 2017). Notwithstanding the acknowledged challenges with respect to reported and recorded rape data, the issues are broadly consistent across the jurisdictions and are not expected to unduly affect the analysis.

However, only England/Wales and Canada report recorded rape offences as a separate category. In their reporting of crime data, New Zealand and Australia do not differentiate between different forms of sexual assault/offences. As a result, New Zealand and Australia have been excluded from this part of the analysis.

Robbery

The *Canadian Criminal Code* (1985, s.343) sets out a comprehensive definition of robbery:

(a) Steals, and for the purpose of extorting whatever is stolen or to prevent or overcome resistance to the stealing, uses violence or threats of violence to a per- son or property;
(b) Steals from any person and, at the time he steals or immediately before or immediately thereafter, wounds, beats, strikes or uses any personal violence to that person;
(c) Assaults any person with intent to steal from him; or
(d) Steals from any person while armed with an offensive weapon or imitation thereof.

Table 6.14 Reported assault, rape and robbery numbers, by country: 2015–2018

Year	Country	Assault	Rape	Robbery
2015	EW	418,261	29,394	50,772
2016	EW	456,991	35,850	55,824
2017	EW	505,244	41,509	74,130
2018	EW	539,767	53,970	82,566
2015	Can	211,832	20,948	22,149
2016	Can	216,498	21,579	21,958
2017	Can	222,688	24,740	22,831
2018	Can	230,698	28,741	22,450
2015	NZ	30,774		3,068
2016	NZ	32,301		3,238
2017	NZ	33,070		3,747
2018	NZ	34,050		3,375
2015	Aus	180,555		8,968
2016	Aus	191,331		9,412
2017	Aus	192,031		9,592
2018	Aus	192,442		10,120

All major crime data sources are set out in note (iv)

Similar definitions apply in England/Wales (*Theft Act* 1968 (UK)), Australia (for example: *Criminal Code* 1899, s.409 (QLD); *Penalties and Sentences Act* 1992 (QLD))[6] and New Zealand (*Crimes Act* 1961, s.234 (NZ)). As such, the offence of robbery is expected to be recorded in a broadly consistent manner.

6.3.6   Other Major Crime Indicators: Analysis by Country

Comparable data has been located at national level for the period 2015–2018. Table 6.14 documents the recorded numbers for each of the three offence categories: assault, rape and robbery. Table 6.15 sets out the same data as a relative rate per 100,000 population. To aid comparison, the relative rates for each offence category are displayed visually in Figs. 6.4, 6.5 and 6.6.

The most notable feature of Table 6.14 is the increase in absolute numbers for each crime category in England/Wales between 2015 and 2018. The number of assaults increases by 29%, rapes by 84% and robberies by 63%. The reasons for these changing rates are not the focus of our analysis, but it is noted that explanations differ.

---

[6]Australia's federal system of governance empowers each state/territory to determine their own criminal law provisions. As Brisbane is located in Queensland, the relevant Queensland legislation has been used in this study.

Table 6.15 Reported assault, rape and robbery rates, per 100,000 population: 2015–2018

Year	Country	Assault	Rape	Robbery
2015	EW	722.57	50.78	87.71
2016	EW	782.77	61.41	95.62
2017	EW	860.08	70.66	126.19
2018	EW	913.06	91.30	139.67
2015	Can	593.37	58.68	62.04
2016	Can	615.93	61.39	62.47
2017	Can	609.44	67.71	62.48
2018	Can	623.51	77.68	60.68
2015	NZ	669.00		66.70
2016	NZ	687.26		68.89
2017	NZ	688.96		78.06
2018	NZ	696.32		69.02
2015	Aus	752.94		37.40
2016	Aus	792.92		39.01
2017	Aus	780.61		38.99
2018	Aus	773.17		40.66

All major crime and population data sources are set out in notes (i) and (iv)

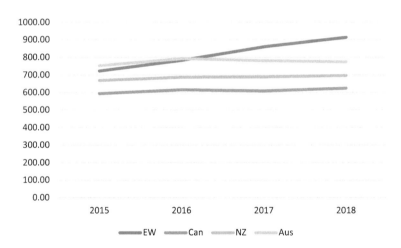

Fig. 6.4 Reported assaults by country per 100,000 population: 2015–2018

Some of the increases may be attributed to better reporting processes and/or increased confidence in police responses (see, for example, Davis and Dossetor 2010; Roberts and Stalans 2018), while others may be a result of the reduction in police numbers

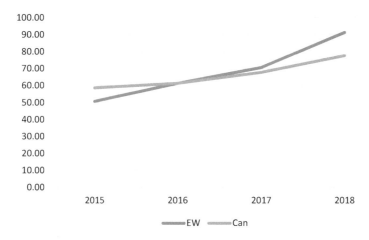

Fig. 6.5 Reported rapes in England/Wales and Canada, per 100,000 population: 2015–18

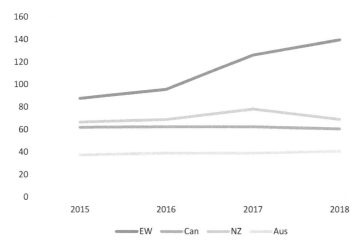

Fig. 6.6 Reported robberies by country per 100,000 population: 2015–2018

in England/Wales noted earlier.[7] The other countries all show some increase, but at a slower rate: Canada recorded minimal increase in robberies, while assaults and rapes increased by 9% and 37% respectively; New Zealand assaults increased by 11% and robberies by 10%; and in Australia assaults increased by 7%, and robberies by 13%.

For assault offences, as depicted in Fig. 6.4, the relative rates are broadly comparable between England/Wales and Australia, although the data for 2018 indicates that rates are starting to diverge. In common with the absolute number of offences, the rate per 100,000 population is increasing more rapidly in England/Wales than in

---

[7]Brogden and Ellison (2012) argue that cutbacks on policing, as a key State service, have had a damaging effect on community well-being.

Australia: 26% between 2015 and 18 compared with 3%. The relative rates in Canada and New Zealand are also broadly comparable. Overall, no statistically significant differences are evident.

For the offence of rape, depicted in Fig. 6.5, comparison is only possible between England/Wales and Canada. Over the four-year period, the relative rate and overall trajectory are broadly similar, although England/Wales has steadily overtaken Canada in relative terms despite starting from a lower rate per 100,000 population. England/Wales increased by 82% compared with 32% in Canada. To understand the diverging trajectories, a range of situational and operational factors would need to be examined to determine whether, for example, the rates reflect more offending or more reporting of offences. For our purposes, for the data examined, there is insufficient evidence to point to a statistically higher risk of rape in England/Wales than in Canada.

The most notable difference for the rate of offending across the four jurisdictions can be seen in relation to robbery, depicted in Fig. 6.6. The rate per 100,000 population in England/Wales is, at times, twice that of Canada and New Zealand, and nearly four times that of Australia. This is the only key crime indicator for which the routinely armed jurisdictions report a consistently lower rate and risk of offending. The data points to a notable and growing issue of reported robbery in England/Wales.

6.3.7 Other Major Crime Indicators: Analysis by City

The same offence categories were examined at city level. Table 6.16 documents the recorded numbers for each of the three categories: assault, rape and robbery. Table 6.17 then sets out the same data as a relative rate per 100,000 population. Once again, to aid comparison, the relative rates for each offence category are displayed visually in Figs. 6.7, 6.8 and 6.9.

In common with the country level analysis, a notable feature of Table 6.16 is the increase in absolute numbers for each crime category in Manchester: the number of assaults increased by 37%, rapes by 213% and robberies by 216%. Again, some of these increases may be attributed to better reporting processes and increased confidence in police responses, and the reasons are not the focus of the analysis here. Brisbane also shows some notable increases, with assaults rising by 34% and robberies by 66%. Toronto recorded only a 2% increase in robberies, while assaults and rapes increased by 14% and 47% respectively. In Auckland recorded assaults and robberies both decreased. The relative rates per 100,000 population, set out in Table 6.17, reflect similar changes.

For assault offences at city level, depicted in Fig. 6.7, there is a marked difference compared with the national data. The relative rates for routinely armed Brisbane and routinely unarmed Auckland are remarkably similar. The rates for routinely unarmed Manchester and routinely armed Toronto are also similar, although notably higher than for Brisbane and Auckland. Manchester and Toronto both follow a similar trajectory, with Manchester over-taking Toronto mid-way through the period under

Table 6.16 Reported assault, rape and robbery numbers by city: 2015–2018

Year	City	Assault	Rape	Robbery
2015	Man	20,930	1,722	3,536
2016	Man	21,886	1,989	4,168
2017	Man	27,525	2,205	6,469
2018	Man	28,581	3,674	7,642
2015	Tor	24,027	3,187	3,462
2016	Tor	25,478	3,651	3,610
2017	Tor	25,913	3,935	3,909
2018	Tor	27,530	4,674	3,527
2015	Auck	2,507		604
2016	Auck	2,384		497
2017	Auck	2,390		618
2018	Auck	2,400		496
2015	Bris	3,648		472
2016	Bris	4,236		469
2017	Bris	4,531		613
2018	Bris	4,881		783

All major crime data sources are set out in note (iv)

Table 6.17 Reported robbery, assault and rape rates, per 100,000 population: 2015–2018

Year	City	Assault	Rape	Robbery
2015	Man	759.43	62.48	128.30
2016	Man	786.70	71.50	149.82
2017	Man	983.39	78.78	231.12
2018	Man	1016.03	130.61	271.67
2015	Tor	850.21	112.77	122.51
2016	Tor	887.43	127.17	125.74
2017	Tor	884.40	134.30	133.41
2018	Tor	931.33	158.12	119.32
2015	Auck	159.68		38.47
2016	Auck	147.71		30.79
2017	Auck	144.24		37.30
2018	Auck	142.52		29.45
2015	Bris	162.86		21.07
2016	Bris	185.55		20.54
2017	Bris	194.46		26.31
2018	Bris	205.08		32.90

All major crime and population data sources are set out in notes (i) and (iv)

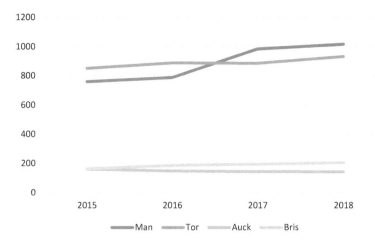

Fig. 6.7 Reported assaults by city per 100,000 population: 2015–2018

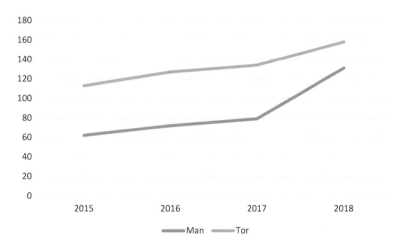

Fig. 6.8 Reported rapes in manchester and Toronto, per 100,000 population: 2015–2018

analysis. From this analysis there is, once again, no evidence to demonstrate a consistently positive effect on community safety of the routine presence of armed police officers.

For the offence of rape, depicted in Fig. 6.8, again comparable data is available only for Manchester and Toronto. The patterns for each city are similar, but the relative rate of reported rape is notably higher in Toronto than in Manchester, although the difference reduced over the period examined.

The offence of robbery again reveals notable differences across the jurisdictions, depicted in Fig. 6.9. Routinely armed Brisbane and unarmed Auckland report very similar levels across the period. Toronto and Manchester again report much higher

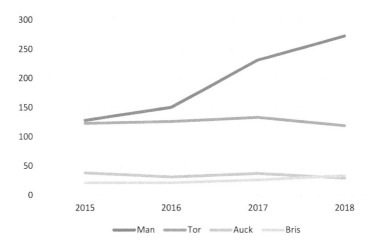

Fig. 6.9 Reported robberies by city per 100,000 population: 2015–2018

levels with routinely unarmed Manchester notably higher and increasingly diverging from armed Toronto. The reported robbery rate per 100,000 population in Manchester is up to nine times that of Brisbane and double that of Toronto. Once again, this is the only key crime indicator for which the routinely armed jurisdictions report a consistently lower rate and risk of offending. The data supports the presence of a notable issue of robbery in England/Wales in general, and Manchester in particular.

As a measure of violence and risk, overall homicide levels are broadly comparable across all jurisdictions, if slightly higher in those deploying routinely armed officers. Other key crime indicators show no notable difference, other than robbery which is much higher in England/Wales and Manchester.

6.3.8 Civilians Fatally Shot by Police

A logical application of the "routinely armed police = safer community" construct is that the presence of routinely armed police officers within a community will be inherently protective, and act as a deterrent, actively discouraging individuals from behaving in a manner which may require a lethal police intervention. The result would be, in theory, fewer fatal police shootings and a safer community.

In our previous analysis, contrary to the assumed community safety benefit of the presence of police firearms, we have found that the jurisdictions in which police officers are routinely armed do not typically report lower levels of serious crime (specifically homicide, robbery, assault and rape). We now expand our examination to include civilians fatally shot by police. We argue that this is a, generally objectively measured, mechanism through which both community and police officer safety can be gauged. The fatal shooting of a civilian presumes a behaviour that is sufficiently

Table 6.18 Number and relative rates of fatal police shootings, by country: 2007–2017

Years	Jurisdiction	Civilians fatally shot by police	Civilians fatally shot by police per 100,000 population
2007–17	England/Wales	22	0.04
2007–17	Canada	260	0.75
2007–17	New Zealand	16	0.36
2007–17	Australia	47	0.20

Fatal police shooting and population data sources are set out in notes (i) and (v)

dangerous—to either the community or the officer themselves—to warrant a lethal intervention. The presumption that police who routinely carry firearms enable and ensure safety (community and/or police) should mean lower numbers of fatal police shootings of civilians in routinely armed jurisdictions.

We have collated and analysed the number of civilians fatally shot by police at a national level for the period 2007–2017, documented in Table 6.18. As annualised data not available for each jurisdiction, the absolute and relative figures are aggregated for the 11 year period.

It is clear that the relative risk of being fatally shot by a police officer is notably higher in Canada than in all other jurisdictions. The risk in Canada is more than twice that in New Zealand, nearly four times that in Australia, and nearly 19 times higher than in England/Wales. The statistical significance of the difference the jurisdictions is confirmed by a Pearson's chi-squared test on the aggregated data:

$$X^2(3 \text{ df}) = 382.75, \text{ (p-value} < 0.001\,[2.2e - 16]).$$

Standardised residuals: England/Wales $= -15.38$; Canada $= 18.88$; New Zealand $= 0.85$; Australia $= -2.69$.

It is reasonable to consider the relative number of sworn police officers (per 100,000 population) as an explanatory variable to help to situate these findings (see Table 6.4). More police on the streets could increase the number of interventions. However, the rate of sworn officers per 100,000 population is lower in Canada (at 198) than England/Wales, Australia and New Zealand (218, 232 and 199 respectively), and we found no correlation with respect to police numbers and fatal police shootings. Therefore, we cannot conclude that a higher number of police officers accounts for the statistically higher number of fatal police shootings in Canada.

We also interrogated the number of civilians fatally shot by police at city level. Comparative data covers a much longer period, 1980–2017, and is set out in Table 6.19. To calculate the rate per 100,000 population, given the range of years covered by the city data, the mean population figure has been adjusted for this analysis. Population data has been sourced for the period 1980–2017 and the mean calculated for each city:

Manchester: 2,497,000; Toronto: 2,515,111; Auckland: 1,171,778; Brisbane: 1,708,556.

Table 6.19 Number and relative rates of fatal police shootings, by city: 1980–2017

Years	City	Civilians fatally shot by police	Civilians fatally shot by police per 100,000 population
1980–2017	Man	1	0.04
1980–2017	Tor	24	0.95
1980–2017	Auck	6	0.51
1980–2017	Bris	19	1.11

Fatal police shooting data sources are set out in note (v)

Manchester recorded only one fatal police shooting across the whole 38-year period. By contrast Toronto, a city of similar population size, recorded 24 fatal police shootings. As the figures for Brisbane are not publicly available for the whole period, they have been extrapolated from data derived from the Coroners Court of Queensland (Queensland Courts 2020). The search term "police shooting" yielded 46 results for the period 2002–2016. Of these, 17 involved the death of a civilian caused by a police firearm, of which 7 occurred in Brisbane. This equates to approximately 0.5 per year. Assuming a broadly equal distribution of fatal shootings across the time period, this would total 19 fatal police shootings between 1980 and 2017. It is recognised that the data for Brisbane is not directly comparable, which limits direct comparison with the other three cities. However, the findings still point to a higher number o f fatal police shootings when compared with Auckland and Manchester.

Overall, at city level, the risk of being fatally shot by a police officer is nearly 24 times higher in Toronto than in Manchester. Both Toronto and Brisbane, the routinely armed jurisdictions, report higher relative rates of fatal police shootings of civilians than the routinely unarmed Manchester and Auckland. The statistical significance of the differences is again confirmed using a Pearson's chi-squared test on the aggregated data:

$$X^2(3 \text{ df}) = 26.867, \text{ (p-value} < 0.001 \, [6.277e - 06]).$$

Standardised residuals: Manchester $= -4.5$; Toronto $= 2.3$; Brisbane $= 3.3$; Auckland $= -1.1$

In common with the national level analysis, using the relative number of sworn police officers as an explanatory variable is insufficient to explain the different numbers and rates of fatal police shootings across the cities. Toronto (194) does have a higher number of sworn officers per 100,000 population than Auckland and Brisbane (53 and 107 respectively), but a lower number than Manchester (254). Once again, we found no correlation with respect to sworn police numbers and fatal police shootings.

The risk of key crime (other than robbery) is not notably lower in the armed jurisdictions, but the risk of being fatally shot by police is much higher. This appears to align with the notion of the "law of the instrument"—whereby the availability of a particular response (such as a police firearm) increases the likelihood that it

Table 6.20 Number of incidents in which police firearms were discharged in England/Wales: 2009–2018

	2009	2010	2011	2012	2013	2014	2015	2016	2017	2018
Number of incidents	6	6	4	4	3	4	6	7	10	12

Non-fatal police shooting data sources are set out in note (vi)

will be used (to shoot someone), even in situations where other solutions may be objectively more appropriate (Horowitz 1962; Kaplan 1964). Our analysis suggests that the presence of a firearm does increase the likelihood of its use, regardless of demonstrable need.

Of course, there is a chance that our analysis is skewed by the focus on fatal police shootings. It is possible that, when called to do so, police in England/Wales discharge their firearms in a less lethal manner. To examine this, we turn our attention to non-fatal police shootings.

6.3.9 Non-fatal Police Shootings: National

Non-lethal firearms use includes the number of times police discharged their firearms with protective intent in the course of their duties. It has not been possible to locate data for each country that is directly comparable, so no inferential analyses have been undertaken. Sufficient data is also not available at city level. It has also not been possible to discern a clear and comprehensive picture of the non-fatal use of firearms by police officers across Canada. In 2015, an attempt to obtain specific data on how often Canadian police officers shoot people returned little information of use (Ling 2015). The project found that few provinces publish data on police use of force, associated injuries or deaths, and requests for information were typically unsuccessful. The number of civilians fatally shot by police is known but, at present, there continues to be no data in the public domain to facilitate a comparative analysis of police firearms discharge and/or associated non-lethal injuries. However, from data that has been obtained for England/Wales, New Zealand and Queensland, Australia, some patterns of note are evident.

In England and Wales, the number of incidents in which conventional police firearms were discharged is published for the years ending March 2009 to March 2018, and is set out in Table 6.20. This data relates to intentional discharges in situations of perceived danger.[8]

Across the ten-year period, firearms were discharged a total of 62 times by police officers in England and Wales. This equates to an average of 6.2 incidents per year: with this figure including fatal and non-fatal shootings.

---

[8]Figures exclude accidental discharges, discharges for animal destruction, and the use of firearms during police training and tyre deflations.

Table 6.21 Number of incidents in which police firearms were discharged in New Zealand: 2017–2018

	2017	2018
Number of police firearms discharge incidents	6	7

Non-fatal police shooting data sources are set out in note (vi)

Table 6.22 Discharge of firearms by the queensland police service: 2000–2014

	Non-fatal discharge	Fatal discharge
2000	0	1
2001	0	0
2002	2	3
2003	4	2
2004	2	1
2005	4	1
2006	4	1
2007	6	2
2008	2	1
2009	5	0
2010	2	0
2011	6	0
2012	5	1
2013	3	1
2014	7	4
TOTAL	**52**	**18**

Non-fatal police shooting data sources are set out in note (vi)

In New Zealand, firearms discharge data is currently only publicly available for 2017 and 2018, as documented in Table 6.21. From this limited dataset, firearms discharge appears to be atypical and constitutes an exceptional response by police officers in New Zealand.

No data could be obtained in relation to the discharge of firearms by police across Australia. However, in 2015 the Queensland Police Service (QPS) published a review of violent confrontations with police (QPS 2015: 20). This report contained data for fatal and non-fatal firearms discharge for the period 2000–2014, which is summarised in Table 6.22.[9]

Across the 15-year period, QPS officers discharged their firearms on 70 occasions (including fatal and non-fatal incidents), which equates to an average of 4.7 firearms discharges per year.

[9]This data also excludes the use of firearms during police training, tyre deflations and animal destructions.

Table 6.23 Comparison of annual firearms discharge incidents, England/Wales and Queensland, Australia

Jurisdiction	Mean annual firearms discharges	Mean annual firearms discharges per 100,000 population
England/Wales	6.2	0.01
Queensland, Australia	4.7	0.1

Non-fatal police shooting data sources are set out in note (vi)

Table 6.24 Discharge of firearms by the Queensland Police Service: Jan–April 2017–2019

	Jan–Apr 2017	Jan–Apr 2018	Jan–Apr 2019
Police firearms discharge incidents	9	9	18

Non-fatal police shooting data sources are set out in note (vi)

Table 6.25 Annual firearms discharge incidents, England/Wales, New Zealand and Queensland, Australia: 2017–2019

	2017	2018	2019	Mean annual firearms discharges (2017–2018)	Mean annual firearms discharges per 100,000 population
England/Wales	10	12	n/a	11	0.02
New Zealand	6	7	n/a	6.5	0.13
Queensland	27	27	54	27	0.54

Non-fatal police shooting data sources are set out in note (vi)

As we have comparable comprehensive data for both England/Wales and Queensland, Table 6.23 sets out the average number of annual firearms discharge incidents per 100,000 population.[10] This reveals that the average annual number of firearms discharges by police, per 100,000 population, is approximately ten times higher in Queensland than in England/Wales.

Additional data was reported for three four-monthly periods in 2017, 2018 and 2019 (Hartley 2019). Again, this refers to the discharge of firearms by police in Queensland, and is summarised in Table 6.24. These figures indicate that the use of firearms by police in Queensland has increased since the publication of the 2015 review.

Assuming a generally steady pattern of firearms discharge across the year, the four-monthly figures have been extrapolated to provide an indication of possible annual numbers, as shown in Table 6.25. An additional, and more direct, comparison

---

[10]The calculation used the 2018 population for England/Wales (59,116,000) and the 2014 population for Queensland (4,780,000)–see note (i).

has then been made with data from England/Wales and New Zealand for the years 2017 and 2018.[11]

The mean annual number of firearms discharge incidents has increased in both England/Wales and Queensland, Australia. However, the rate per 100,000 of population is now 27 times higher in routinely armed Queensland than in routinely unarmed England/Wales, and four times higher than in routinely unarmed New Zealand.

It is apparent that armed police responders in England/Wales successfully avoid discharging their weapons in almost every case. The exceptions are so few as to run into single figures in most years—despite being the most populous jurisdiction examined. While detailed consideration sits outside of the specific focus of this paper, it is reasonable to ponder why armed police officers in England/Wales are so successful in avoiding the need to discharge their weapons. One obvious factor is their higher level of training; armed officers are a specialist role in England/Wales, and training is intensive and ongoing (Police Firearms Officers Association 2020). At the same time, though, due to the routinely unarmed nature of policing in England/Wales, armed police only attend where circumstances necessitate—likely to be situations of the highest risk. As such, the discharge averse nature of the armed police response is all the more remarkable.

We have found that, overall, the rate of police firearms discharge is notably higher in Queensland, Australia than in both England/Wales and New Zealand. Given the findings for fatal police shootings of civilians, it is concerning that comparable data is not available for Canada.

6.3.10 Other Non-lethal Uses of Force: Conducted Energy Devices

To expand our analysis, we examined the use of another non-lethal weapon: conducted energy devices (CEDs, also known as tasers). The deployment of CEDs to frontline police officers has steadily increased over the last decade (Dymond 2018; Marsh et al. 2019). CEDs were first trialled in England/Wales in 2003 and rolled out to all police forces by 2013 (BBC 2019). In New Zealand, CEDs were first used in 2006 and rolled out to all frontline police vehicles in 2010 (NZ Government 2009). The roll-out of CEDs to all Queensland police officers commenced in January 2009 (QPS 2009).

Data has been located regarding the use of CEDs across England/Wales, New Zealand and in Queensland, Australia. Once again, sufficient data was not available for Canada, or for the four cities within the scope of our study.

CED use and discharge in England/Wales, for the period 2011–2017, is set out in Table 6.26. CED use and discharge in New Zealand is set out in Table 6.27, this time for the period 2014–2018. A more limited set of data is available for Queensland,

---

[11]The calculation used the 2018 population for England/Wales (59,116,000) and New Zealand (4,890,000), and the 2018 population for Queensland (4,988,000)—see note (i).

Table 6.26 CED use by police in England/Wales: 2011–2017

	CED incidents	CED fired	% Incidents where CED discharged	Incidents per 100,000 population
2011	7877	1506	19.12	14.02
2012	8161	1620	19.85	14.43
2013	10,380	1733	16.70	18.23
2014	10,095	1733	17.17	17.58
2015	10,390	1729	16.64	17.95
2016	11,294	1755	15.54	19.35
2017	17,084	1872	10.96	29.08

CED use data sources are set out in note (vii)

Table 6.27 CED use by New Zealand Police: 2014–2018

	CED Incidents	CED Discharged	% Incidents where CED discharged	Incidents per 100,000 population
2014	1014	108	10.65	22.48
2015	998	126	12.63	21.70
2016	1290	296	22.95	27.45
2017	1189	186	15.64	24.77
2018	1075	210	19.53	21.98

CED use data sources are set out in note (vii)

Australia for the period 2012–2014, and is reported in Table 6.28. To enable more meaningful comparison, the number of incidents during which a CED was used (threatened, aimed or fired) has also been calculated per 100,000 population and is included in each table.

In the one year for which comparative data is available, 2014, the number of CED incidents per 100,000 population was 17.58 in England/Wales, 22.48 in New Zealand, and 40.36 in Queensland. The rate in Queensland was nearly twice that of New Zealand and over double the rate in England/Wales. This shows that, in addition to higher rates of firearms use, CED usage is also notably higher in routinely armed Queensland than in the non-routinely armed jurisdictions of England/Wales and New Zealand.

Table 6.28 CED Use by Queensland Police: 2012–2014

	CED Incidents	Incidents Per 100,000 Population
2012	816	17.89
2013	1553	33.33
2014	1929	40.36

CED use data sources are set out in note (vii)

6.3.11   *Police Deaths: National*

A key measure of police safety in any jurisdiction is the number and rate of non-accidental police deaths. For example, in their assessment of the dangerousness of policing, White et al. (2019) analysed police deaths in the USA between 1970 and 2016.

Accurate data for each of the jurisdictions is recorded within their respective police memorial websites. Each site documents the cause of each police officer death. Any non-intentional (such as a vehicle or other accident) or health related deaths have been excluded from the analysis. We have extracted and examined the non-accidental police officer deaths (at national and city level), as a reasonable measure of police officer safety. If police officer safety is notably lower in any jurisdiction, we would expect this to be reflected in a higher rate of police officer non-accidental deaths. To provide a further analytical dimension, we have identified the number of deaths by firearms for each jurisdiction.

Before we set out our findings, we acknowledge suicide as another form of non-accidental police death. Sufficient data in relation to police officer suicide is not available for each jurisdiction and, as a result, we have not included suicide within our analysis. We also recognise that each individual suicide will reflect a wide and complex set of drivers—for which establishing a correlation with community and/or officer safety would be inappropriate. Had the data been available, we could have examined any use of police issued firearms in the commission of suicide. However, any findings and associated conclusions would lack essential context. Crucially, we would not be able to establish whether the suicide would have occurred without the availability of a firearm. For these reasons, suicide is excluded from our analysis.

Comprehensive data is available for non-accidental police deaths in each national jurisdiction for the period 1980–2018. In Table 6.29 we set out the total number of non-accidental police deaths, the number of officers fatally shot, the mean annual number of non-accidental deaths, and the rate per 100,000 sworn officers. Given the longer period covered by the aggregated non-accidental death data, the mean sworn police personnel numbers as set out in Table 6.2 have been re-calculated. Sworn

Table 6.29   Police non-accidental deaths for each national jurisdiction: 1980–2018

	Police deaths	Police shot	% Police shot	Mean annual police deaths	Mean annual number of sworn police officers (1980–2018)	Police death rate per 100,000 sworn officers
England/Wales	63	24	38	1.62	127,450	1.27
Canada	79	66	84	2.03	60,102	3.38
New Zealand	8	6	75	0.21	6,743	3.04
Australia	47	37	79	1.21	42,719	2.83

Police non-accidental death data sources and police personnel data are set out in notes (ii) and (viii)

police numbers were located for selected years between 1980 and 2018 (as not all years were available) and the mean figures was calculated for each jurisdiction.

Canada (84%) and Australia (79%) both record higher percentages of non-accidental police deaths by firearm, than New Zealand (75%) and England/Wales (38%). Using the annualised data, the mean number of non-accidental police deaths per year is highest in Canada (2.03), followed reasonably closely by England/Wales (1.62) and Australia (1.21). New Zealand records notably lower numbers of non-accidental police deaths (0.205)—nearly ten times lower than Canada, eight times lower than England/Wales, and six times lower than in Australia. However, when these absolute figures are re-framed within the number of sworn police officers, a different picture is evident.

Canada continues to record the highest rate of non-accidental police deaths (3.38 per 100,000 sworn officers), followed by New Zealand (3.04). Australia recorded a rate of 2.83 per 100,000 sworn officers, and England/Wales a rate of 1.27. This analysis reveals that the likelihood of a non-accidental police death (as a proportion of sworn officers) is two and a half times higher in the routinely armed jurisdiction of Canada than in the routinely unarmed location of England/Wales. The rates in Australia and New Zealand are broadly similar, and both are more than twice that of England/Wales.

A further test sought to establish the statistical significance of these differences. As the data for non-accidental police deaths has been collated in aggregated form (1980 to 2018), a Pearson's chi-squared test compared the rate of non-accidental deaths across the four jurisdictions.

$$X^2(3 \text{ df}) = 28.269, \text{ (p-value} < 0.001 \, [3.189e - 06]).$$

Standardised residuals: England/Wales $= -6.1$; Canada $= 4.8$; Australia $= 2.1$; New Zealand $= 1$.

The analysis indicates that England/Wales has a significantly lower rate of non-accidental police deaths than the other jurisdictions. Both Canada and Australia have significantly higher rates than England/Wales and New Zealand. Not only are police officers in Canada and Australia more likely to be shot and killed, they are also more likely to be killed by any means while on duty. As such, police in both routinely armed jurisdictions do not appear to be safer than the unarmed officers in England/Wales or New Zealand.

6.3.12 Police Deaths: City

Comprehensive data is available for each city for the period 1980–2018. In Table 6.30 we set out the total number of non-accidental police deaths, the number of officers fatally shot, the mean annual number of non-accidental deaths, and the rate per 100,000 sworn officers. Again, given the longer period covered by the aggregated non-accidental death data, sworn police numbers were located for selected years

Table 6.30 Non-accidental police officer deaths in each city: 1980–2018

	Police Deaths	Police Shot	% Police Shot	Mean Annual Police Deaths	Mean Annual Number of Sworn Police Officers (2014–2018)	Police Death Rate per 100,000 sworn officers
Manchester	7	2	29	0.18	6,913	2.60
Toronto	5	4	80	0.13	5,380	2.42
Auckland	1	1	100	0.03	797	3.76
Brisbane	4	4	100	0.10	2,323	4.30

Police non-accidental death data sources and police personnel datat are set out in notes (ii) and (viii)
In one of the Toronto deaths, the police officer's own firearm was used to kill

between 1980 and 2018 (as not all years were available) and the mean figure was calculated for each jurisdiction.

Toronto (80%), Auckland (100%) and Brisbane (100%) all record higher percentages of non-accidental police deaths by firearm than Manchester (29%). Using the annualised data, the average number of non-accidental police deaths per year is highest in Manchester (0.18), followed by Toronto (0.13) and Brisbane (0.10). Auckland recorded the lowest rate, at 0.03 non-accidental deaths per year, six times lower than Manchester, four times lower than Toronto and three times lower than Brisbane. When these absolute figures are re-framed within the number of sworn police officers, once again, a very different picture is evident. Brisbane now records the highest rate of non-accidental police deaths (4.3 per 100,000 sworn officers), followed by Auckland (3.76). The rate in Manchester (2.60) and Toronto (2.42) were broadly consistent with each other. This data yielded no results of statistical significance.

Overall this analysis reveals mixed findings. The cities most and least likely to record non-accidental police deaths were those where officers are routinely armed. What this suggests, once again, is an absence of the presumed protection afforded to routinely armed officers.

6.3.13 Police Injury

An obvious extension of our analysis of non-accidental police deaths is to examine the number, type and rate of injuries sustained by police officers while on duty. Unfortunately, data in relation to police injury is not sufficiently comparable across the jurisdictions. Our experience is typical. Gibbs (2019) noted that the rigorous study of violence against police officers, other than that with fatal outcomes, is rare and generally lacking from policing literature. A police death is measured objectively and consistently, and recorded comprehensively, whereas police injuries are more subjectively assessed, selectively recorded, and may be subject to privacy consid-erations. As a result, we have not included analysis of police injuries within this study.

6.4   Chapter Conclusion

As a measure of violence and risk, overall homicide levels are broadly comparable but slightly higher in the routinely armed jurisdictions. Other key crime indicators show no notable difference, other than robbery which is much higher in England/Wales. By contrast, the rate of fatal police shootings is significantly higher in the armed jurisdictions of Canada, Toronto and Brisbane, although not Australia as a whole. The difference in the key crime indicators is not sufficient to explain the far higher number of fatal police shootings. While there is no discernible increase in homicide-related risk in the armed jurisdictions of Canada and Australia, there is a more notable difference in the rates of homicides which are committed using a firearm—with rates in the armed jurisdictions five times higher than in the unarmed. Once again, this difference, while statistically significant, is not sufficient to fully account for the even greater variance in the rates of fatal police shootings.

With respect to more general discharge of firearms, and the use of conducted energy devices, the data points to lower use in the non-routinely armed jurisdictions. For other measures of police safety, the rate of non-accidental police deaths is higher in routinely armed Canada than routinely unarmed England/Wales. In the cities, the differences were more nuanced. Overall, police officers in Canada, in particular, do not appear to be safer than in England/Wales or New Zealand.

It is evident from our analysis that both Canada and England/Wales occupy posi-tions at either extreme across the measures examined. Australia and New Zealand are much closer for some of the relative measures we have compared: rate of fatal police shootings of civilians; homicide rate; gun-related and other homicide rates, assault, rape, robbery. Indeed, some risks are slightly higher in routinely unarmed New Zealand than in routinely armed Australia. We are not seeking to explain this—we highlight these findings to ensure transparency and to inform our ongoing research.

From the measures we have analysed, what we can state as a clear and repeated finding is the absence of definitive evidence to support the contention that routinely arming police officers inevitably and invariably increases community or police safety (whether by deterring violent crime, creating a level of reassurance, or through higher levels of effective police intervention). If we compare the two largest juris-dictions, Canada and England/Wales, other than for robbery, the latter appears to be notably "safer". Homicide levels are not only lower in England/Wales, the rate of fatal police shootings is approximately 18 times lower than in Canada. The rates of all three measures in New Zealand and Australia are much more comparable. However, overall, our analysis has found insufficient empirical evidence to support the expectation that routinely arming police officers increases safety.

With respect to each fatal police shooting of a civilian, what we are not able to elucidate from the raw data is their precise nature or their appropriateness. If we use overall homicide rates as a broad indicator of the risk of violence, there are no notable differences between the four jurisdictions. For robbery, England/Wales records a notably higher rate, yet this is not matched by a higher rate of fatal police shootings. Each of the four jurisdictions applies an expectation of minimum force in their policing interactions. In Canada, for example, the first two of six prescribed principles within the National Use of Force Framework, (Canadian Association of Chiefs of Police [CACP] 2000: 3) are: (1) *The primary responsibility of a peace officer is to preserve and protect life*; (2) *The primary objective of any use of force is to ensure public safety.* A fatal police shooting is, arguably, the antithesis of minimum force. Yet the risk posed to civilians by police officers is significantly higher in Canada than all other jurisdictions. Canada appears to be a clear example of the effects of the law o f he instrument (Horowitz 1962; Kaplan 1964).

We do not offer any explanation for the patterns within our data; that is not our purpose. However, from our analysis, we can start to provide an empirically-informed challenge to the assumption that the routine presence of armed police increases and ensures community safety and/or police safety. That there are differences within and between the jurisdictions further undermines a "universal truth" that armed police make us safer. We reiterate our acknowledgement that causal linkages cannot and should not be discerned from the method that has been adopted, and that the findings set out here are not broadly generalisable.

Nevertheless, our findings provide an evidence-based challenge to calls to arm police in currently unarmed jurisdictions. Given the basic human right of civilians to be safe, any change to policing practice which may affect this right must be demonstrably justified. There may be good reasons to move towards the routine deployment of armed officers, but an inevitable increase in safety is not one of them.

Notes

(i)   **Population data has been derived from the following sources for each jurisdiction**:
      England/Wales and Manchester:
      Office for National Statistics (UK), England Population—mid-year estimate, https://www.ons.gov.uk/peoplepopulationandcommunity/populationan dmigration/populationestimates/timeseries/enpop/pop [accessed 15 October 2019].
      Office for National Statistics (UK), Wales Population—mid-year estimate, https://www.ons.gov.uk/peoplepopulationandcommunity/populationan dmigration/populationestimates/timeseries/wapop/pop.
      Office for National Statistics (UK), Population Estimates, https://www.ons.gov.uk/peoplepopulationandcommunity/populationandmigration/populatio nestimates [accessed 4 December 2019].

Australia and Brisbane:
Australian Bureau of Statistics, Australian Historical Population Statistics, https://www.abs.gov.au/AUSSTATS/abs@.nsf/DetailsPage/3105.0.65.0012016?OpenDocument [accessed 15 October 2019].

Canada and Toronto:
Statistics Canada, Total Population, https://www150.statcan.gc.ca/n1/en/subjects/population_and_demography/census_counts/total_population [accessed 17 October 2019].

Archived Demographic Estimates by Census Division, https://www150.statcan.gc.ca/t1/tbl1/en/tv.action?pid=1710008401 [accessed 4 December 2019].

Toronto, At a Glance, https://www.toronto.ca/city-government/data-research-maps/toronto-at-a-glance/ [accessed 4 December 2019].

New Zealand and Auckland:
Statistics New Zealand, Population, https://www.stats.govt.nz/topics/population [accessed 18 October 2019].

Population of Auckland, https://figure.nz/chart/SJ55NQw8yzlKHUOn [accessed 4 December 2019].

(ii) **Sworn police personnel data has been derived from the following sources for each jurisdiction**:

England/Wales and Manchester
Police Work Force England and Wales Statistics, https://www.gov.uk/government/collections/police-workforce-england-and-wales [accessed 15 October 2019].

Police Work Force Data England and Wales, Second Edition, https://www.gov.uk/government/statistics/police-workforce-england-and-wales-31-march-2019 [accessed 20 February 2020].

Police Numbers in England and Wales, https://fullfact.org/crime/police-numbers/ [accessed 15 October 2019].

Australia and Brisbane:
Report on Government Services, 2019, https://www.pc.gov.au/research/ongoing/report-on-government-services/2019/justice/police-services (Attachment Tables, Table 6A.3) [accessed 15 October 2019].

Source Book of Australian Criminal and Social Statistics 1804–1988, https://aic.gov.au/publications/archive/source-book-Australian-criminal-social-statistics_1804-1988 (page 137) [accessed 15 October 2019].

Police Source Book, https://aic.gov.au/sites/default/files/publications/archive/downloads/police-source-book.pdf (Table 3.1) [accessed 15 October 2019].

Sworn Police Officers in Australia, https://aic.gov.au/publications/cfi/cfi116 [accessed 15 October 2019].

Year Book Australia, 2002, https://www.abs.gov.au/AUSSTATS/abs@.nsf/Previousproducts/712FAED4666FABD2CA256B35001967CE?opendocument [accessed 15 October 2019].

Police Services, https://www.pc.gov.au/research/ongoing/report-on-govern
ment-services/2013/2013/09-government-services-2013-chapter6.pdf (Table
6A) [accessed 15 October 2019].

Australian Social Trends, 1997, https://www.abs.gov.au/AUSSTATS/abs@.
nsf/2f762f95845417aeca25706c00834efa/a4d719473be50fdfca2570ec001
b2c95!OpenDocument [accessed 15 October 2019].

Canada and Toronto:

Police Personnel and Selected Crime Statistics, https://www150.statcan.gc.
ca/t1/tbl1/en/tv.action?pid=3510007601 [accessed 15 October 2019].

TPS Annual Statistical Report 2016, https://www.torontopolice.on.ca/public
ations/files/reports/2016statsreport.pdf (page 43) [accessed 15 October 2019].

TPS Annual Statistical Report 2012,
https://www.torontopolice.on.ca/publications/files/reports/2012statsreport.
pdf (page 5) [accessed 15 October 2019].

CBC, Toronto Police Under-staffed, https://www.cbc.ca/news/canada/
toronto/toronto-police-morale-staffing-critical-association-1.4458139
[accessed 15 October 2019].

New Zealand and Auckland:

New Zealand Police Annual Report, 2017–2018, https://www.police.govt.
nz/sites/default/files/publications/annual-report-2017-2018.pdf [accessed 15
October 2019].

New Zealand Police Annual Report, 2013, https://www.police.govt.nz/
sites/default/files/publications/annual-report-2013.pdf [accessed 15 October
2019].

Annual Statistics (section 14 of each report), https://www.police.qld.gov.au/
maps-and-statistics/annual-statistics [accessed 15 October 2019].

Long Term Data Series, Social Indicators, https://archive.stats.govt.nz/bro
wse_for_stats/economic_indicators/NationalAccounts/long-term-data-ser
ies/social-indicators.aspx (C1.4) [accessed 20 February 2020].

(iii) **Homicide data has been derived from the following sources for each
jurisdiction**:

England/Wales and Manchester

Office for National Statistics (UK), Appendix Tables: Homicide in England
and Wales, https://www.ons.gov.uk/peoplepopulationandcommunity/cri
meandjustice/datasets/appendixtableshomicideinenglandandwales (Table 1)
[accessed 15 October 2019].

UK Home Office, Statistical Bulletin: Homicides, Firearms and Intimate
Violence 2010/11,
https://assets.publishing.service.gov.uk/government/uploads/system/upl
oads/attachment_data/file/116483/hosb0212.pdf [accessed 15 October
2019].

Crime in England and Wales, Police Force Area Data Tables, https://www.
ons.gov.uk/peoplepopulationandcommunity/crimeandjustice/datasets/police
forceareadatatables [accessed 25 November 2019].

Australia and Brisbane:
Australian Institute of Criminology, Homicide in Australia, https://www.cri mestats.aic.gov.au/NHMP/ [accessed 15 October 2019].
Australian Bureau of Statistics, Recorded Crime, Victims, 2018, https://www.abs.gov.au/AUSSTATS/abs@.nsf/DetailsPage/4510.02018?OpenDocument [accessed 15 October 2019].
Australian Institute of Criminology, Trends in Homicide 1980/90–2013/14, https://www.crimestats.aic.gov.au/NHMP/1_trends/ [accessed 15 October 2019].
Australian Institute of Criminology, Victims of Violent Crime by Weapon Type 2010–2017, https://crimestats.aic.gov.au/facts_figures/1_victims/A3/ [accessed 15 October 2019].
Queensland Crime Statistics, https://mypolice.qld.gov.au/queensland-crime-statistics/ [accessed 10 November 2019].

Canada and Toronto:
Statistics Canada, Number and Rate of Homicide Victims, https://www150.statcan.gc.ca/t1/tbl1/en/cv.action?pid=3510007101#timeframe [accessed 17 October 2019].
Statistics Canada, Number and Percentage of Homicide Victims, https://www150.statcan.gc.ca/t1/tbl1/en/cv.action?pid=3510007201#timeframe [accessed 17 October 2019]
Statistics Canada, Firearm Related Violent Crime, https://www150.statcan.gc.ca/n1/pub/85-005-x/2018001/article/54962-eng.htm [accessed 17 October 2019].
Statistics Canada, Police Reported Crime Statistics 2018, https://www150.statcan.gc.ca/n1/pub/85-002-x/2019001/article/00013-eng.htm [accessed 17 October 2019].
Statistics Canada, Method Used to Commit Homicide 2000–2010, https://www150.statcan.gc.ca/n1/pub/85-002-x/2011001/article/11561/tbl/tbl03-eng.htm [accessed 17 October 2019].
Analytics and Information, https://app.powerbi.com/view?r=eyJrIjoiNmFiNjgyYzYtMjlhZi00ODA4LThkNjgtNDZmZWFjYjhhY2IyIiwidCI6Ijg1MjljMjI1LWFjNDMtNDc0Yy04ZmI0LTBmNDA5NWFlOGQ1ZCIsImMiOjN9 [accessed 10 November 2019].
Homicides by Selected Type of Weapon, by Census Metropolitan Area, 1999 to 2008, https://www150.statcan.gc.ca/n1/pub/85-002-x/2010001/article/11146/tbl/tbl05-eng.htm [accessed 10 November 2019].

New Zealand and Auckland:
New Zealand Police, Police Statistics on Homicide Victims in New Zealand 2007–2016,
https://www.police.govt.nz/sites/default/files/publications/homicide-vic tims-report-2017.pdf [accessed 18 October 2019].
New Zealand Police, Historic Murder Offences 1926–2017, https://www.police.govt.nz/sites/default/files/publications/historic-new-zealand-murder-rates.pdf [accessed 18 October 2019].

Stuff.NZ, The Homicide Report, https://interactives.stuff.co.nz/2019/the-homicide-report/data.html [accessed 18 October 2019].

(iv) **Data relating to reported robberies, assaults and rape has been derived from the following sources for each jurisdiction**:
England/Wales and Manchester:
UK Crime Statistics, https://www.ukcrimestats.com/Police_Force/Greater_Manchester_Police [accessed 10 December 2019].
Crime in England and Wales, Police Force Area Data Tables, https://www.ons.gov.uk/peoplepopulationandcommunity/crimeandjustice/datasets/policeforceareadatatables [accessed 30 November 2019].
Domestic Abuse, Rape and Sexual assault, https://www.gmp.police.uk/police-forces/greater-manchester-police/areas/greater-manchester-force-content/sd/stats-and-data/domestic-abuse-and-rape-sexual-assault/ [accessed 10 February 2020].
Sexual Offending, Home Office Appendix Tables, https://www.ons.gov.uk/peoplepopulationandcommunity/crimeandjustice/datasets/sexualoffendinghomeofficeappendixtables [accessed 10 February 2020].
Canada and Toronto:
Toronto Police Service, Crime App, https://torontops.maps.arcgis.com/apps/webappviewer/index.html?id=300d35778c114ef49d59454225043681 [accessed 4 October 2019].
Toronto Police Service, Public Safety Data Portal, https://data.torontopolice.on.ca/pages/catalogue [accessed 4 October 2019].
Incident Based Crime Statistics, https://www150.statcan.gc.ca/t1/tbl1/en/tv.action?pid=3510017701&pickMembers%5B0%5D=1.1&pickMembers%5B1%5D=2.34 [accessed 10 October 2019].
Police Reported Crime Rate, 2007–2017, https://www150.statcan.gc.ca/n1/pub/85-002-x/2018001/article/54974/t/tbl01b-eng.htm [accessed 10 October 2019].
Violent Crime, https://www150.statcan.gc.ca/n1/pub/85-005-x/2018001/article/54962-eng.htm [accessed 19 October 2019].
Australia and Brisbane:
Queensland Police Service, Annual Statistics, https://www.police.qld.gov.au/maps-and-statistics/annual-statistics [accessed 11 November 2019].
Queensland Crime Statistics, https://mypolice.qld.gov.au/queensland-crime-statistics/ [accessed 11 November 2019].
ABS, Recorded Crime: Victims, 2018, https://www.abs.gov.au/AUSSTATS/abs@.nsf/DetailsPage/4510.02018?OpenDocument [accessed 11 November 2019].
Crime Statistics Agency (Vic), Recorded Offences, https://www.crimestatistics.vic.gov.au/crime-statistics/historical-crime-data/year-ending-31-december-2018/recorded-offences [accessed 10 February 2020].

New Zealand and Auckland:

Proceedings (offender demographics), https://www.police.govt.nz/about-us/publications-statistics/data-and-statistics/policedatanz/proceedings-offender-demographics [accessed 10 February 2020].

New Zealand Police, Victimisations, https://www.police.govt.nz/about-us/publications-statistics/data-and-statistics/policedatanz/victimisations-demographics [accessed 10 February 2020].

(v)   **Police shooting data has been derived from the following sources for each jurisdiction: England/Wales and Manchester**:

Wikipedia, List of Killings by Law Enforcement Officers in the UK, https://en.wikipedia.org/wiki/List_of_killings_by_law_enforcement_officers_in_the_United_Kingdom [accessed 15 October 2019].

Australia/Queensland and Brisbane:

Queensland Courts, Findings: Coroner's Court, https://www.courts.qld.gov.au/courts/coroners-court/findings [accessed 16 April 2020].

Australian Institute of Criminology, Police Shootings in Australia, https://aic.gov.au/publications/sr/sr13 [accessed 15 October 2019].

Queensland Police (2015). *Violent Confrontations Review.* [Online] Queensland Police Service, https://www.police.qld.gov.au/corporatedocs/reportsPublications/Documents/QPS%20Violent%20Confrontations%20Review.pdf [accessed 10 November 2018].

Canada and Toronto:

Huffington Post, 'Canada Needs A National Database To Track Deadly Force By Police', https://www.huffingtonpost.ca/erick-laming/deadly-force-by-police_a_23034831/?utm_hp_ref=ca-police-shooting/ [accessed 17 October 2019].

Wikipedia, List of Killings by Law Enforcement Officers in Canada, https://en.wikipedia.org/wiki/List_of_killings_by_law_enforcement_officers_in_Canada#cite_note-64 [accessed 17 October 2019].

USA Today, 'Video in Toronto Killings Shows a Divide Between U.S. and Canada on Deadly Force', https://www.usatoday.com/story/news/2018/04/26/video-toronto-killings-shows-divide-between-u-s-and-canada-deadly-force/551798002/ [accessed 17 October 2019].

Toronto Police, Annual Report, https://www.torontopolice.on.ca/publications/files/reports/crm2018annualreport.pdf [accessed 10 November 2019].

New Zealand and Auckland:

New Zealand Herald, 'Chronology of Fatal Shootings by NZ Police', https://www.nzherald.co.nz/nz/news/article.cfm?c_id=1&objectid=10539110 [accessed 18 October 2019].

Radio New Zealand, 'Police Shootings Number 29 in Last 65 Years', https://www.radionz.co.nz/news/national/280368/police-shootings-number-29-in-last-65-years [accessed 18 October 2019].

Stuff.NZ, Under Fire, https://interactives.stuff.co.nz/2017/11/under-fire/ [accessed 18 October 2019].

(vi) **Police non-fatal shooting and firearms discharge data has been derived from the following sources for each jurisdiction**:
England/Wales:
Home Office, Police use of firearms, England and Wales: April 2017 to March 2018 data tables (Table 4), https://assets.publishing.service.gov.uk/government/uploads/system/uploads/attachment_data/file/728507/police-use-firearms-statistics-england-and-wales-april-2017-to-march-2018-hos b1518.pdf (page 6) [accessed 20 October 2019].
Australia/Queensland:
Queensland Police Service, Violent Confrontations Review, https://www.police.qld.gov.au/sites/default/files/2018-12/QPS%20Violent%20Confrontations%20Review.pdf (page 20) [accessed 20 October 2019].
Hartley, A. (2019), from https://www.abc.net.au/news/2019-06-20/research-why-queensland-police-drawing-firearms-more-often/11216284 [accessed 20 October 2019].
New Zealand:
New Zealand Police Tactical Options Research Report, 2018, from https://www.police.govt.nz/sites/default/files/publications/annual-tactical-options-research-report-7.pdf [accessed 20 October 2019].
New Zealand Police Tactical Options Research Report, 2017, from https://www.police.govt.nz/sites/default/files/publications/annual-tactical-options-research-report-6.pdf [accessed 20 October 2019].

(vii) **Police CED use data has been derived from the following sources for each jurisdiction**:
England/Wales:
Police Use of Force Statistics, England and Wales, April 2017–March 2018, from https://www.gov.uk/government/statistics/police-use-of-force-statistics-england-and-wales-april-2017-to-march-2018 (and reports for earlier years) [accessed 30 October 2019].
Police Use of Conducted Energy Devices, from https://www.gov.uk/government/statistics/police-use-of-taser-x26-conducted-energy-devices-statistics-england-and-wales-1-january-to-31-december-2016-data-tables [accessed 30 October 2019].
Australia/Queensland:
Queensland Police Service, Violent Confrontations Review, https://www.police.qld.gov.au/sites/default/files/2018-12/QPS%20Violent%20Confrontations%20Review.pdf (page 22) [accessed 20 October 2019].
New Zealand:
New Zealand Police Tactical Options Research Report 2018, from https://www.police.govt.nz/sites/default/files/publications/annual-tactical-options-research-report-7.pdf [accessed 30 October 2019].
New Zealand Police Tactical Options Research Report 2017, from https://www.police.govt.nz/sites/default/files/publications/annual-tactical-options-research-report-6.pdf [accessed 30 October 2019].

New Zealand Police Tactical Options Research Report 2016, from https://www.police.govt.nz/sites/default/files/publications/annual-tactical-options-research-report-5.pdf[accessed 30 October 2019].

New Zealand Police Tactical Options Research Report 2015, from https://www.police.govt.nz/sites/default/files/publications/annual-tactical-options-research-report-4.pdf [accessed 30 October 2019].

New Zealand Police Tactical Options Research Report 2014, from https://www.police.govt.nz/sites/default/files/publications/annual-tactical-options-research-report-3.pdf [accessed 30 October 2019].

(viii) **Police non-accidental death data has been derived from the following sources for each jurisdiction**:

England/Wales: 1980–2018

UK Police Roll of Honour, from https://www.policememorial.org.uk/rollof honour.php# [accessed 8 October 2019].

Canada: 1975–2018 (removed deaths from the period 1975–1979)

CBC, 2018 Four Decades of Police Homicides, from https://www.cbc.ca/news/canada/manitoba/4-decades-of-canadian-police-homicides-by-the-numbers-1.4781581 [accessed 8 October 2019].

Canada Police Roll of Honour, from https://www.thememorial.ca/memorial/index/honourrollprofile?hid=646 [accessed 8 October 2019].

Australia: 1980–2018

Australia Police Honour Roll, from https://npm.org.au/honour-roll/ [accessed 8 October 2019].

New Zealand: 1980–2018

NZ Police Roll of Honour, from https://www.police.govt.nz/sites/default/files/publications/remembrance-day-booklet-2018.pdf [accessed 8 October 2019].

References

Allen, W. D. (2007). The reporting and under-reporting of rape. *Southern Economic Journal, 73*(3), 623–641.

BBC. (2019). Taser use by police in England and wales reaches record high. *BBC News*, 20 December. Retrieved from: https://www.bbc.com/news/uk-50862398

Becker, G. S. (1968). Crime and punishment: An economic approach. *Journal of Political Economy, 76*, 169–217.

Brogden, M., & Ellison, G. (2012). *Policing in an age of austerity: A post-colonial perspective.* Oxon: Routledge.

CACP. (2000). *A National Use of Force Framework* [online]. Retrieved from: https://www.cacp.ca/cacp-use-of-force-advisory-committee-activities.html?asst_id=199 [Accessed 25 November 2019].

Davis, B., & Dossetor, K. (2010). (Mis) perceptions of crime in Australia. *Trends and Issues in Crime and Criminal Justice*, no. 396. Canberra: Australian Institute of Criminology.

Delehanty, C., Mewhirter, J., Welch, R., & Wilks, J. (2017). Militarization and police violence: The case of the 1033 program. *Research and Politics, 4*(2), 1–7.

Dymond A. (2018). 'Taser, Taser'! Exploring factors associated with police use of Taser in England and Wales. *Policing and Society*,https://doi.org/10.1080/10439463.2018.1551392.

Ehrlich, I. (1972). The deterrent effect of criminal law enforcement. *The Journal of Legal Studies, 1*(2), 259–276.

Funnell, A. (2019). Why the creeping militarisation of our police has experts worried. *ABC News Online*, 20 September. Retrieved from: https://www.abc.net.au/news/2019-09-20/creeping-milita risation-of-police-why-experts-are-concerned/11517266.

Gibbs, J. C. (2019). Rhetoric versus reality of decreasing danger for police over time. *Criminology and Public Policy, 18*(1), 7–10.

Goldsworthy, T. (2014). Urban combat: Ferguson and the militarisation of police. *The Conversation*, 19 August.

Gray, E., Jackson, J., & Farrall, S. (2011). In search of the fear of crime: Using interdisciplinary insights to improve the conceptualisation and measurement of everyday insecurities. In D. Gadd, S. Karstedt, & S. Messner (Eds.), *Sage Handbook of Criminological Research Methods*. London: Sage Publications.

Hartley, A. (2019). Queensland police are firing their weapons more often as frontline threat increases. *ABC News Online*, 20 June. Retrieved from: https://www.abc.net.au/news/2019-06-20/research-why-queensland-police-drawing-firearms-more-often/11216284.

Horowitz, M. J. (1962). Trends in education: report on the annual meeting of the American Educational Research Association (AERA) held 19–21 Feb 1962, *Journal of Medical Education, 37* (June): 634 .

Jacobs, B. A. (2010). Deterrence and deterrability. *Criminology, 48*(2), 417–441.

Kaplan, A. (1964). *The conduct of inquiry: Methodology for behavioural science*. San Fransisco: Chandler Publishing Co.

Kraska, P. B. (2007). Militarisation and policing: Its relevance to 21st Century police. *Policing: a Journal of Policy and Practice, 1*(4), 501–513. Retrieved from: https://academic.oup.com/pol icing/article-abstract/1/4/501/1440981.

Lehner, E. A. (2017). Rape process templates: A hidden cause of the underreporting of rape. *Yale Journal of Law and Feminism, 29*(1), 207–240.

Ling, J. (2015). It's impossible to find out exactly how many people are shot by cops in Canada. *Vice News*, 21 Aug. Retrieved from: https://www.vice.com/en_us/article/j59peb/its-impossible-to-find-out-exactly-how-many-people-are-shot-by-cops-in-canada.

Mann, H., Garcia-Rada, X., Hornuf, L., & Tafurt, J. (2016). What deters crime? Comparing the effectiveness of legal, social, and internal sanctions across countries. *Frontiers in Psychology 7*, Article 85.

Marsh, S., Dodd, V., & Grierson, J. (2019). Police chiefs criticise £10m taser roll out. *The Guardian*, 28 Sept. Retrieved from: https://www.theguardian.com/uk-news/2019/sep/27/police-in-england-and-wales-to-be-given-more-tasers-in-10m-rollout?CMP=Share_AndroidApp_Tweet.

Matthews, S. K., & Agnew, R. (2008). Extending deterrence theory: Do delinquent peers condition the relationship between perceptions of getting caught and offending? *Journal on Research in Crime and Delinquency, 45*(2), 91–118.

McGrath, A. (2009). Offenders' perceptions of the sentencing process: A study of deterrence and stigmatisation in the New South Wales Children's Court. *Australian and New Zealand Journal of Criminology, 42*(1), 24–46.

Mouzos, J. (2003). Australian homicide rates: A comparison of three data sources. *Trends and Issues in Crime and Criminal Justice, 261*(July). Canberra: AIC.

Mummolo, J. (2018). Militarization fails to enhance police safety or reduce crime but may harm police reputation. *Proceedings of the National Academy of Sciences., 115*(37), 9181–9186.

Nagin, D., & Greg, P. G. (2001). Integrating celerity, impulsivity, and extra-legal sanction threats into a model of general deterrence: Theory and evidence. *Criminology, 39*(4), 865–892.

Nanavaty, B. R. (2015). Addressing officer crisis and suicide: Improving officer wellness. *FBI Law Enforcement Bulletin*, Retrieved from: leb.fbi.gov/articles/featured-articles/addressing-officer-crisis-and-suicide-improving-officer-wellness.

NZ Government. (2009). *$10 million to complete national taser roll out* [press release]. Retrieved from: https://www.beehive.govt.nz/release/budget-2009-judith-collins-10-million-complete-national-taser-roll-out.

Osse, A., & Cano, I. (2017). Police deadly use of firearms: An international comparison. *The International Journal of Human Rights, 21*(5), 629–649.

Police Firearms Officers Association. (2020). *Police Firearms Officers Association.* [Online], England/Wales. Retrieved from: https://www.pfoa.co.uk.

QPS. (2009). *Review of the Queensland Police Service taser trial.* Retrieved from: https://www.cabinet.qld.gov.au/documents/2009/jun/qps%20taser%20trial/Attachments/Review%20of%20QPS%20Taser%20Trial.pdf.

QPS. (2015). *QPS Violent Confrontations Review.* Queensland Police Service. Retrieved from: https://www.police.qld.gov.au/sites/default/files/2018-12/QPS%20Violent%20Confrontations%20Review.pdf (p. 20).

Queensland Courts. (2020). *Findings: Coroner's Court.* Retrieved from: https://www.courts.qld.gov.au/courts/coroners-court/findings.

Richardson, N. J., Barrick, K., & Strom, K. J. (2019). Is policing safer today? *Criminology and Public Policy, 18*(1), 37–45.

Roberts, J. V., & Stalans, L. J. (2018). *Public opinion, crime and criminal justice.* New York: Routledge.

Tonry, M. (2008). Learning from the limitations of deterrence research, In M. Tonry (Ed.), *Crime and justice: A review of research* (pp. 279–312). University of Chicago Press: Chicago.

UNODC. (2014). *Global study on homicide 2013.* Vienna: UNODC.

Von Hirsch, A., Bottoms, A. E., Burney, E., & Wikstrom, P.-O. (1999). *Criminal deterrence and sentence severity: An analysis of recent research.* Oxford: Hart Publishing.

White, M. D., Dario, L. M., & Shjarback, J. A. (2019). Assessing dangerousness in policing. *Criminology and Public Policy, 18*(1), 11–35.

Chapter 7
'The Devil's Right Hand': Policing, Media and Weapons Product Placement

Abstract An evidence-based assessment of correlations between the presence of firearms in routine policing and measures of safety is only part of the picture. Police capacity and inclination to use force do not operate in isolation. Legislative, organisational, procedural, situational and individual choices all inform collective priorities and on-the-ground officer decisions, but they are also a product of community perception and expectation. This brings to the fore the tropes and constructs of popular culture—and the media, in all its forms. From where is the belief in the beneficial effect of routinely armed policing derived? Why is it that in routinely unarmed jurisdictions, a typical response to issues of mass public disorder, changes in offending behaviours or individual high-profile crimes is "just give the police guns"? Why is their such widespread belief that more ready police access to lethal force leads to better outcomes, for both police and the community? We have established that empirical evidence is minimal, and our study has failed to find any notable positive association between the routine arming of police officers and safety. In this chapter we apply a range of research literature, media examples and case studies to an exploration of fictional media traditions, and the positioning of firearms within dramatic narrative arcs and public sentiment more generally. We reflect on the power of product placement and media priming on perceptions of the use of firearms by police officers in fictional dramas, and the influence this can have on real-world policing. We argue that Weapons Product Placement, the deliberate and extensive inclusion of firearms across screen content, has a subtle and wide-ranging influence on policing styles. We draw these elements together to consider the ways in which the fictional media shape expectations about the need for police to have guns, and influence the belief that having a gun is an essential and positive aspect of policing.

7.1 Introduction

Lone Survivor is an American-made action movie, released in 2013, which depicts a real-life, unsuccessful military operation by US Navy SEALs in Afghanistan. The movie was a commercial success and was generally favourably reviewed, indeed hailed as "one of the most realistic war movies of all time" (Cummings and Cummings 2014). Despite the approbation, a particular choice of props created controversy. The Navy SEALs were depicted armed with M9 Beretta pistols, rather than the SIG-P226, which was the corps' standard issue at the time. This deviation from the historical record was entirely due to product placement, negotiated by the marketing firm Brand-In Entertainment. According to Fox News, Beretta paid a rumoured US$250,000 for the firm's guns to be used (McKay 2014). The intent was to boost the status of Beretta generally, and sales of its pistols in particular.

This affair may seem minor, and on one level it is. There is a sub-culture of people who care a great deal about the makes and models of firearms which appear on screen, and who devote significant time, energy and expertise to documenting and sharing their knowledge. One example is the Internet Movie Firearms Database (IMFD), a crowd-sourced wiki (IMFD 2020). IMFD lists the weapons which appear in literally thousands of movies and television programs with impressive attention to detail. In such forums, the plausibility or otherwise of a particular gun in a particular filmed setting can generate heated debate.

In the broad scheme of popular culture and its workings in society, the make of a prop gun is of no great interest. But the controversy over *Lone Survivor* and the Beretta has wider implications. It gives an insight into the, sometimes murky, world of "product placement"—the use of products and brand identities in screen content, often paid for in cash or kind, in the hope of influencing audience consumer choices. While any particular instance of product placement may be trivial, taken collectively product placement can have a significant influence on behaviours and popular understandings, a process often referred to as "priming" (Balasubramanian et al. 2006; Law and Braun-La Tour 2003; Surette 2015).

It is our contention that what we will call Weapon Product Placement (WPP) is an aspect of popular culture which merits considerably more attention than it has received to date. Though the details are usually kept confidential, WPP is a common-place of screen production in the United States, and, like product placement more generally, is increasing (Chen and Wang 2016). The reach and influence of American popular culture, particularly on other Anglophone societies, is immense (Jacobs and McKernan 2008). This is exemplified by exposure to American made movies and television shows, and also extends to the world of gaming (Curtin and Shattuc 2018; Higson et al. 2015; Pohlmann 2019). Even where separate national screen industries exist, these will often follow American models and/or offer American content alongside local productions. As a result, WPP originating in the United States has a potential real-world influence that can extend globally. WPP can affect and shape how the public expect police to act, to respond to threat, to resolve conflict, and even whether and how police officers should look with respect to their uniform and the carriage and type of weapons.

In this chapter we examine the role and effect of product placement, with a focus on television drama and movies.[1] We reflect upon the example of tobacco and relate

---

[1]News media, whether in legacy or new media forms, and social media in its many platforms and manifestations, are also important, but they are not examined in this chapter.

key models and contextual framing to the less well understood effects of WPP. We explore the dominance of American-made fictional drama in general, and crime focused drama in particular, and consider the broader effects of both upon the public consciousness in relation to policing and the use of firearms by police. We examine the theoretical and applied basis for such effects, through priming, scripting, narrative persuasion and cultivation theory. Finally, we acknowledge the gun itself as a form of media and consider how and why this affects the use and perception of firearms by police officers—both in dramatic fiction and in the real world.

7.2 Product Placement

The genesis of product placement in feature films is often said to be the 1982 Steven Spielberg-directed movie *E.T.*, whose eponymous hero eats a Hershey brand confectionary, the sales of which then soared (Adler 1999: 246). Any student of cinema recognises that the practice is much older, going back to at least the 1930s, albeit more ad hoc and more likely to be paid in kind than in cash (Karniouchina et al. 2011). Nevertheless, the commercial possibilities of product placement became more fully recognised from the 1980s, driven by the reality that it was less expensive and often more effective than conventional advertising. For example, Adler (1999) explains that Hershey did not pay for the use of their product in *E.T.*, but agreed to a promotion in which Hershey would include mention of the movie in its advertising. By the 1990s, almost every major production had product placement as a significant part of its budget (Fuchs 2005). It was routine practice for scripts to be reworked to incorporate products whose marketers were helping to pay the bills (Gardner 2014; Palmer 1998). In the years since, as media has evolved, product placement has moved with it—into video games, music videos, song lyrics and social media (Hilgard et al. 2016). Branded consumer goods, such as cars, mobile phones, laptops and sunglasses, are promoted widely and purposefully via such product placement (Truth Initiative 2018).

The great benefit to marketers of product placement is that it "sneaks past the normal defences that consumers erect against advertising and makes even controversial product uses appear normal and desirable, often glamorous" (Adler 1999: 248). That said, as product placement has become more common, media audiences have become more alert to it. A number of studies have found that the more overt and obvious product placement is, the less successful at influencing consumer behaviour it is likely to be (Cowley and Barron 2008; Finlay et al. 2005; Kuhn et al. 2010). Considerable research has been devoted to identifying the most effective way of placing products in order to maximise marketing impact (Karniouchina et al. 2011). While this is obviously of interest to marketing professionals and the firms for which they work, that is not our concern here. Overt product placement is largely harmless (Grzyb et al. 2018; Hudson and Elliott 2013). It is the less visible scripts and understandings which underlie product placement which are potentially more concerning and directly relevant to our thesis.

7.2.1 Product Placement: The Example of Tobacco

It is useful to position our examination of the less visible scripts and contextual effects of product placement by first looking at a product which has received considerable research attention, and the perception and depiction of which has undergone transformative public, legal and political pressure: tobacco.

"The past is a foreign country," L.P. Hartley famously observes, "they do things differently there" (Hartley 1958: 1). Old movies confirm it. One example of literally thousands, is the 1987 movie *House of Games*, an American psychological noir-thriller directed by David Mamet.[2] It was a modest success at the time, and remains an interesting and clever exploration of deception and self-deception. But what startles the viewer today is the amount and frequency of smoking. The main character, the apparently respectable psychologist Dr. Margaret Ford, smokes like the proverbial chimney. We know her brand, Camels, because of all the cigarette packets artfully placed in shot. The smoking does relate to characterisation—Ford is an expert on the addictions of others; rather less astute about her own—but that could have been conveyed in many other ways. And, Ford aside, pretty much everyone else smokes. The movie is dark, edgy, full of sexual frisson. The overall subtext is that smoking is sophisticated, perhaps a bit risky, but certainly alluring.

In the 1980s, the extent of tobacco use in *House of Games* was wholly unremarkable. Smoking was commonplace across public and private domains, and tobacco product placement in movies and television drama was widespread (Jamieson and Romer 2010). The specific financial details were usually kept confidential, but court hearings and public inquiries exposed the arrangements for a number of productions. To take just a few examples: Brown and Williamson Tobacco spent nearly US$1,000,000 over four years to feature its cigarettes in more than 20 movies (Levin 1994); in the 1987 James Bond movie *Licence to Kill*, Philip Morris paid US$350,000 for Bond to smoke Lark cigarettes (Coombs et al. 2011); the makers of the first three Christopher Reeves *Superman* movies (released in 1978, 1980 and 1983) accepted money to promote Marlboro cigarettes (Coombs et al. 2011). Superman himself does not smoke, but Lois Lane does, and the hero flies through a landscape dotted with Marlboro billboards. Many more such deals are documented, and a great many must have escaped legal scrutiny.

The tobacco industry worked hard to place their products, with a simple rationale: to create demand and to increase sales. Their choice of movies was far from accidental. Those intended for youth audiences, such as *Superman*, were a particular target. Young audiences were tempting for tobacco manufacturers, because most people who become long-term smokers begin the habit as teenagers (Adler 1999). Popular culture, especially screen drama, was a significant factor in making teenagers more likely to begin smoking. The portrayal of smokers was typically positive, with

---

[2]The examples discussed in this chapter are illustrative. We acknowledge that there are, of course, numerous movies and television shows that depict similar behaviours. Our purpose here is not to offer a comprehensive analysis of the prevalence and effect of tobacco use in fictional drama, but to highlight relevant trends, issues and changes.

smoking associated with success and acceptance (Adler 1999: 257). Smoking was presented as common-place and aspirational, and smokers as role-models—with demonstrable effects upon young viewers in particular (Fuchs 2005).

Through the late 1980s and 1990s, general awareness of the harmful effects of tobacco became more definitive and accepted. Despite this, smoking in American movies and television shows continued to increase during the early 1990s (Stockwell and Glantz 1997). In response, several high-profile law suits steadily narrowed the circumstances in which tobacco use could be depicted on screen (Cummings and Proctor 2014; Keller et al. 2004). A complex series of legal proceedings and court rulings culminated in the 1998 Master Settlement Agreement (MSA), by which the tobacco industry was bound (among many other things) not to:

> make, in the connection with any motion picture made in the United States, or cause to be made any payment, direct or indirect, to any person to use, display, make reference to, or use as a prop any cigarette, cigarette package, advertisement for cigarettes, or any other item bearing the brand name, logo, symbol, motto, selling message … or any other indicia of product identification … (Adler 1999:.265).

The visibility of specific brands on screen is secondary to the normalised presence of tobacco more generally. The problem with *House of Games* is not that the protagonist smokes Camels, but that she and so many other characters smoke at all. The harm caused by the presence of tobacco in movies and on television is rooted in the cumulative effect of hundreds or thousands of productions which glamorised and normalised smoking and, as result, validated its use (Leonardi-Bee et al. 2016).

The MSA brought hope that depictions of tobacco use on screen would decline, and while the tobacco industry has successfully exploited various loopholes, there has indeed been some reduction (Eagle and Dahl 2018; Lyons et al. 2013) particularly in mainstream US television and cinema (Glantz et al. 2010; Jamieson and Romer 2010; Greenhalgh et al. 2020). This reduction in the visibility of tobacco use correlates with lower numbers of smokers, particularly across primarily English-speaking nations (Greenhalgh et al. 2020: Chap. 2). We do not claim that the MSA and its consequences is the only explanation for reduced rates of smoking and associated illness and premature death. However, the recognition of tobacco product placement as a public health issue, concomitant public concern and pressure, and a drive to develop laws and industry codes to reduce tobacco use on screen, is clearly a key part of the picture.

We have only briefly explored tobacco product placement. Our purpose here is to provide an applied comparison with WPP. While not an exact fit, we posit that similar models and contextual research findings may apply to the much less researched issue of WPP.

7.2.2 Weapon Product Placement

While its meaning varies greatly, a firearm is everywhere symbolically powerful (Blanchfield 2019). It is, as Haag puts it "a culturally charged object … totem … there will always be anecdotal evidence to corroborate a variety of feeling toward guns, from love to revulsion" (Haag 2016: xvii). Both extremes are present in American media, from company websites to popular music.

On its website, the SIG Saur company (motto: "Never Settle") commits itself to selling high quality firearms, accessories and training: "We do this because we share the same drive to be the best, the same love of freedom, the same unwillingness to compromise—as those who choose SIG" (SIG 2020).

At the far pole, in a popular song, musician Steve Earle sings of a teenage boy who sees a pistol in the local store:

I saw my first pistol in the general store … when I was thirteen.

I thought it was the finest thing I ever had seen.

I asked, if I could have one when I grew up.

Mama dropped a dozen eggs and she really blew up … I didn't understand.

Mama said, the pistol is the Devil's right hand.

(Earle 1988).

Squarely in the SIG Saur corner is US made fantasy movie *The Matrix*.

The Matrix (the first of a trilogy of movies) depicts a titanic struggle between the forces of evil and a tiny band of resistance fighters. The hero, Neo, is the unlikely hope of the resistance. He is a white-collar office worker, pale, fearful, and unaware of his special status. One day he receives an envelope, in it is a mobile phone. The envelope is clearly labelled Federal Express. The phone is a Nokia, its logo unmissable. These are the only two brand-names in an otherwise featureless, unlabelled and unremarkable office setting, and the effect is almost comic.

Much later, Neo has joined the resistance and with the help of his comrade Trinity he endeavours to rescue the resistance leader, who is being held captive in a tower block. Together, they shoot their way into the building, in what is known as the "Lobby Scene" (Young 2010). Neo is unrecognisable as the pallid office worker of earlier in the movie: he has realised his destiny, become a man, and he is armed to the teeth. Product placement is again at work. According to the IMFD, the list of guns used in the scene includes pistols and machine-pistols made by Beretta, Uzi, Heckler and Koch and a sub-machine gun of Yugoslav manufacture, the Skorpion (IMFD 2020). The guards and soldiers who are slaughtered have more prosaic, though still deadly, weapons: Smith and Wesson revolver, M16 carbines, Franchi semi-automatic shotguns. The narrative underpinning the Lobby Scene is age-old: a vast evil is afoot and those responsible are holding a hostage. The friends of the hostage enter evil's centre of power (in narrative studies it is called "the inmost cave") and, though vastly outnumbered, use calculated violence to rescue the hostage and defeat evil (Booker 2004: 17–30; Campbell 1969). Young (2010: 26) observes that, at the end of the scene "[t]he lobby is devoid of corpses, encouraging the spectator to feel exhilarated rather than disturbed". The storyline is so familiar that it would be a surprising, even disconcerting, action movie which did *not* contain a set-piece shoot- 'em-up of this type. And it is *there*, in the storylines and moral constructs which are needed for WPP to be viable, that WPP does the most harm. Mirroring the previous ubiquity of on-screen tobacco use, the problem with WPP is not any particular brand of gun. It is the fact of guns, as a product, being used to solve a problem, to resolve a confrontation, to defeat evil—over and over and over.

Firearms feature in approximately 60% of Hollywood movies and many are well-known brands (Fierman 1999). WPP continues to be extraordinarily prevalent particularly in American produced screen content, including mainstream television and cinema. To take one example from broadcast television: the inaugural season of the American Broadcasting Company television drama *The Rookie*, a police procedural set in Los Angeles and first broadcast in the United States in October 2018. In the three-minute official trailer for the show's pilot, a gun is held, raised or fired twenty times: once every nine seconds. Table 7.1 lists the identifiable weapons which appeared on screen across the first season, which comprised 20 episodes (IMFD 2020).

Unfortunately, using IMFD it is not possible to consistently assess how often each gun model appears on screen. However, prominently featured as the weapons carried by regular police officers in *The Rookie* are the Smith & Wesson M&P, the Glock 17, and Remington shotguns. SWAT officers use Colt M4A1 assault rifles. Criminals, like the hapless guards in the Matrix Lobby, are usually armed with older, less-glamorous weapons.

The Rookie is in no way exceptional. In the US ratings period for broadcast television, September 2018-May 2019, ten of the 30 top-rated programs were police or crime-related dramas (Porter 2019). All ten of these dramas feature WPP. For the most recent completed season of each of the ten programs, Table 7.2 documents the number of identifiable firearms, and the most prominent brands, as catalogued by the IMFD. Again, IMFD data does not allow reliable calculation of how often firearms

Table 7.1 Identifiable weapons appearing in season one of The Rookie

Pistols and Revolvers:	*Rifles and Carbines*:
• Beretta 92FS	• AK-103
• Colt Commander	• Blaser R93 Sniper rifle
• Colt Detective Special	• Colt Model 933
• Colt M1911A1	• DSA SA58 OSW
• Colt M1911A1 (Custom Engraved)	• M1 Garand
	• M4A1 Carbine
• Colt MK IV Series 80	
• Colt Mustang	*Shotguns*:
• Colt New Service	• Mossberg 590
• Colt Officer's ACP	• Remington 870 (Magpul MOE handguard)
• CZ 75 P-07 Duty	• Remington 870 (Police Magnum Extended)
• Glock 17	
• Heckler & Koch USP	*Submachine Guns*:
• Ruger KP89	• Heckler & Koch MP5K
• SIG-Sauer P229 (Two-Tone)	• Heckler & Koch MP7A1
• SIG-Sauer P229R	• The SIG-Sauer MPX
• Smith and Wesson 39	
• Smith and Wesson M&P	
• Smith and Wesson M&P Compact	

Data source: IMFD (2020)

appear in each program. However, the number of different brands of firearm used across a particular season can stand as a rough proxy: the more brands depicted, the more prevalent WPP is likely to be.

The following depictions have been excluded from the table: unidentified weapons; military-only weapons which would not realistically be used by police or criminals (such as grenade launchers and aircraft-mounted machine guns); and weapons which appear incidentally, in photographs or shop windows.

From this simple analysis, we can see the normalised presence and use of firearms in many popular US dramas, and the consequential prevalence of WPP. Mirroring the role played by tobacco, the type and brand of firearm matters less than their visibility and the way in which they are integral to the plot and the behaviours of police officers. It is almost expected that officers will automatically draw their weapon in any given interaction, particularly in an environment that is unfamiliar or in the presence of an unknown individual. This normalisation of firearms in broadcast television sets an expectation, consciously or otherwise, of "how policing is done".

Over the past decade, the dominance of broadcast television has been increasingly challenged by digital services. Many of the most successful and influential dramas are now delivered via streaming platforms. Examples include *Narcos, Peaky Blinders, House of Cards* and *The Crown*—dramas made in the United States or the UK, but streamed internationally via Netflix. The streaming trend is likely to continue as new services come online, viewer expectations change, and traditional channels diversify (ENP Newswire 2019; Gilbert 2019).

Netflix, the largest provider of English language streaming content, both purchases and develops its own programming. By the end of 2019, the number of paying Netflix subscribers, globally, was in excess of 167 million, 61 million of whom were located in the United States (Statista 2020). In 2019, Netflix generated revenue of more than US\$20 billion (Netflix Investors 2020). Accurate viewer data on streaming is difficult to obtain, as there are currently no independently audited measures available. While the limitations of self-reported figures are acknowledged, there is no reason to doubt the broad truth about which of its programs Netflix claims to be successful.

According to Netflix, the platform's ten most-viewed programs in the period 2013–2019 were those summarised in Table 7.3 (Gajanan 2019). A notable feature of the list is the continued popularity of crime: eight of the top ten programs have a crime theme. Of these, five frequently feature high levels of gun violence and WPP. Identifiable brands include Beretta, Colt, Glock, Heckler and Koch, Remington and SIG-Sauer (IMFD 2020). Netflix sources content from many different countries, but in a reflection of the dominance of American screen production the Spanish-made *Money Heist (La Casa de Papel)*, is the only non-American production in the top ten list, set out below.

Table 7.2 Top rating police dramas and the number and types of identifiable firearms across the season, from the list of top 30 rated programs September 2018–May 2019

Ratings ranking	Program	Season	Pistols and revolvers	Rifles and carbines	Other	Prominent brands	Notes
3	NCIS	16	11	3		Colt Glock Heckler and Koch SIG-Sauer Smith and Wesson	There is also an NCIS video game. In the game, there are 27 different branded models of firearm
7*	Blue Bloods	9	3			Colt Glock Kahr	This may be an undercount: an earlier season (5) showed 6 pistols, 1 assault rifle and a submachine gun
7*	FBI	1	1			Glock	This may be an undercount
11	Chicago Fire	7	7	2	1 brand of taser	Colt Heckler and Koch SIG-Sauer Smith and Wesson	Chicago Fire is primarily focussed on the fire service rather than police, although many situations require police support/follow-up. As part of the One Chicago NBC offering, the storylines can also cross-over and characters regularly interact with those from Chicago PD (ranked # 15)

(continued)

Table 7.2 (continued)

Ratings ranking	Program	Season	Pistols and revolvers	Rifles and carbines	Other	Prominent brands	Notes
13	Bull	3	4	2		Colt Glock SIG-Sauer Smith and Wesson	Bull is primarily a court-based/justice-driven drama
15	Chicago P.D	6	7			Beretta Glock SIG-Sauer Springfield Armory	
17	NCIS: New Orleans	5	21	16	8 brands of submachine gun 8 brands of shotgun	Beretta Colt Glock Heckler and Koch IMI Uzi Mossberg SIG-Sauer Smith and Wesson	

(continued)

Table 7.2 (continued)

Ratings ranking	Program	Season	Pistols and revolvers	Rifles and carbines	Other	Prominent brands	Notes
22*	Hawaii Five-0	9	21	19	8 brands of submachine gun 8 brands of shotgun 1 brand of taser	Beretta Colt Glock Heckler and Koch IMI Uzi Mossberg SIG-Sauer Smith and Wesson	
22*	NCIS: Los Angeles	10	19	17	9 brands of submachine gun 6 brands of shotgun	Beretta Colt Glock Heckler and Koch IMI Uzi Mossberg SIG-Sauer Smith and Wesson	
26*	9-1-1	2	2			Colt Glock	This focuses on the handling and aftermath of 911 calls and involves all types of emergency responders, not just police

*Depicts equal ranking
Data Sources: IMFD (2020); Porter (2019)

Table 7.3 Ten most viewed Netflix shows, 2013–2019

Ranking by viewer numbers	Netflix show	Crime theme	Gun violence/WPP
1	*Orange is the New Black* (2013–2019)	Y	
2*	*Murder Mystery* (2019)	Y	
3	*Stranger Things* (2016–2019)	Y	Y
4	*Triple Frontier* (2019)	Y	Y
5	*The Perfect Date* (2019)		
6	*Bird Box* (2018)	Y	Y
7	*The Umbrella Academy* (2019)	Y	
8	*Money Heist (La Casa De Papel)* (2017–2019)	Y	Y
9	*Tall Girl* (2019)		
10	*The Highwaymen* (2019)	Y	Y

*A change to how Netflix calculates viewer numbers later elevated a different drama, *The Witcher* (2019), to the number 2 ranking. This has not been included in the analysis here
Data Source: Gajanan (2019)

7.2.3 The Cultural Dominance of US Fictional Drama

Most of the media examples examined so far in this chapter are American. This reflects a simple, stark truth. As Jacobs and McKernan (2008) put it:

> That American television has achieved a position of global dominance is not in question … American television has been the most successful provider of new content for the ever-expanding global commercial television sector… Any discussion of the prospects for a "global" or transnational civil society must take into account this important fact. (Jacobs and McKernan 2008: 1–3).

That this dominance influences broader popular culture is self-evident. Of particular interest to our study is the potential effect on perceptions and expectations of policing in general, and of the routine need for and use of firearms in particular. We return to the four jurisdictions examined in Chap. 6: England and Wales, Canada, Australia and New Zealand (for the next part of the analysis, we position England and Wales in the broader context of the United Kingdom—reflecting the role and structures of broadcasting in that nation).

The relative influence of American screen productions varies between the four locations, with the effect tempered by the extent of homegrown fictional drama in each nation. The United Kingdom imports a range of American, Australian and other international programming, but locally produced television drama dominates to an extent unmatched elsewhere in the Anglophone world. UK audiences share the enthusiasm for crime drama. Of the 10 dramas which drew the largest viewing figures in 2018, five had policing or crime as their core focus (Broadcasters' Audience

Research Board 2019). The top ranked program, *Bodyguard*, was also the one which most had the "look and feel" of US policing dramas.[3] Though set in Britain, where operational police are not routinely armed, *Bodyguard* focusses on anti-terrorism. It includes multiple violent action scenes, and key characters carry and use firearms. In the 2018 season, there are identifiable brands of four handguns, four rifles and 1 submachinegun (IMDB 2020). Three of the four other policing dramas in the top 10 viewer list, *Vera* (ranked 5), *Silent Witness* (6), and *Death in Paradise* (8) feature firearms from time to time, but most commonly in the hands of offenders. The police officers and investigators do not carry or use firearms, and firearms are not integral to the drama. The final drama, *McMafia* (ranked 7), focuses on international organised crime and is set in many different parts of the world. Nevertheless, the presence or use of firearms is still not frequent, and again certainly not integral to the drama.

US derived drama and movies are, of course, still popular in the UK. But the number and popularity of much less violent home-grown police and crime drama is notable. Successful UK crime shows, such as *Sherlock*, *Broadchurch*, *Line of Duty*, and *Happy Valley* can be violent and confronting, but include the visible presence or police use of firearms by exception. Weapons have never been an integral part of solving crime in UK dramas—as the content of more iconic productions such as *Prime Suspect, Inspector Morse, Poirot, Taggart*, and *A Touch of Frost* attest. This reflects and reinforces broader cultural norms whereby the presence of firearms, in both drama and real life, is not normalised; it is not expected and not regarded as necessary.

The importance of popular culture, including screen drama, to successful policing has long been recognised in the United Kingdom. McLaughlin (2005) discusses the importance of the 1950 film *The Blue Lamp*, in the portrayal of English police in popular imagination. He argues that the film's hero, PC George Dixon, epitomised minimum force policing, the iconic "bobby on the beat". This ideal remains enormously popular:

> The police constable... the foundation stone of English policing and a key symbol of "Englishness." can be found in virtually every tourist gift shop in London, in a bewildering number of formats. Postcards, key rings, puppets, dolls, teddy bears, coffee mugs, t-shirts all carry this instantly recognizable image of the English police. An avuncular "bobby" has even featured on the front page of brochures for holidays in London … The English "bobby" has been culturally constituted through a set of storylines which underscore his essential "difference" from the police officers of other countries (McLaughlin 2005: 11–12).

Though here reduced to tourist kitsch, McLaughlin reminds us of the importance of popular culture depictions of policing, and their circular nature. Minimum force policing in the community, doubtless idealised, is reflected and celebrated in UK popular culture, which reinforces and legitimises minimum force policing in the community. As we argue below, the same is true of popular culture and the armed tradition of policing.

---

[3]*Bodyguard* was first broadcast by the BBC, and subsequently made available for streaming via Netflix.

American-made drama productions are more dominant in the other three juris-dictions. In Canada, fears of local identity and culture being swamped by the media of its influential neighbour have led to the imposition of quotas for locally produced content (Ali 2017: 11–14). Canadian broadcasting policy includes a requirement for "maximum use of Canadian creative and other resources in the creation and presen-tation of programming" (Parliament of Canada 2014). However, most local material sits within the domain of news and current affairs, and American content dominates both broadcast and subscription television drama (Ali 2017: 14; Claus 2017).

Australian broadcasters also have to meet local content quotas (Australian Communications and Media Authority 2020), and locally-made police and crime dramas have enjoyed some success. Examples include *Blue Heelers*, *Jack Irish* and the *Underbelly* series, which focused on organised crime in Australia. UK drama is also widely available across Australian television networks, primarily through the Australian Broadcasting Corporation (ABC), the national broadcaster (ABC 2020). However, in recent years Australian commercial broadcast television has become increasingly dominated by American content outside the fields of sport, news and "reality" programs (Quinn 2020; Pascoe 2012). Streaming services, which have no local content restrictions, are even more dominated by American content (Australian Government 2020).

Despite having a relatively small population, New Zealand has for many years been successful in creating locally-produced television and cinema, including the crime dramas *Outrageous Fortune* and *Westside,* and the police procedural *The Brokenwood Mysteries* (Alves 2018; Dunleavy and Joyce 2011). In 2018, among the top ten most viewed programs broadcast in New Zealand were *Border Patrol,* a local real-life show focussing on customs and immigration enforcement, and *Highway Cops*, another documentary style show featuring New Zealand Police at work on the roads (McKenzie 2018). As the officers are filmed in action in real time, they typi-cally do not carry firearms, but do have visible conducted energy devices (tasers) on their belts. As elsewhere, the increased availability of a cornucopia of screen enter-tainment delivered digitally has created fears that programming reflecting a New Zealand identity, including policing styles, will becoming increasingly less viable (Dunleavy and Joyce 2011).

Despite variations between the four nations, it is a reasonable proposition to argue that American-made drama (whether broadcast, streamed or in movie format), makes a significant social and cultural impact across each jurisdiction. One important effect is that American depictions of policing, the use of firearms (by officers and offenders), and embedded WPP are commonplace across popular fictional dramatic offerings. In much the same way as the use of tobacco, police with firearms and firearms more generally are normalised across US television and film drama.

Firearms legislation, gun ownership and use vary across the four jurisdictions. Evans, Farmer and Saligari (2016) compare key provisions and firearms-related data in Australia, the United States and the United Kingdom. However, reliable data for gun ownership is difficult to obtain, particularly where weapons may not be legally held. Table 7.4 summarises key data for our four jurisdictions and the USA.

Table 7.4 Estimated civilian and law enforcement firearms possession by national jurisdiction, 2017

	Estimate of firearms in civilian possession	Estimate of law enforcement held firearms	Population estimate 2017	Estimate of civilian firearms per 100 persons	Ratio estimated civilian: law enforcement firearm possession
Canada	12,708,000	103,000	36,626,000	34.7	123:1
Australia	3,573,000	69,000	24,642,000	14.5	52:1
New Zealand	1,212,000	13,000	4,605,000	26.3	93:1
England/Wales	2,731,000	28,000	58,877,000	4.6	98:1
USA	393,347,000	1,016,000	326,474,000	120.5	387:1

Data Source: This data is derived from the Small Arms Survey (2017), an independent research project run under the auspices of The Graduate Institute of International and Development Studies, in Geneva, Switzerland.

The potential use of firearms in the commission of crime or as a means of self-harm is understandably a cause for concern in all four jurisdictions. However, while there are variations in degree, there is a general absence of expectation of ready civilian access to firearms. Legal and procedural restrictions on access ensure that the opportunities for firearm-related harms are relatively contained. According to the Small Arms Survey (2017), in England and Wales, there are fewer than five firearms for every 100 people. In Canada, the most firearm friendly of the four jurisdictions, there are fewer than 35 firearms per 100 people.[4]

The situation in the United States is vastly different. A combination of lax regulation, long-standing and deeply embedded assertions of the individual right to bear arms, and the existence of several overlapping "gun cultures" has produced a situation where there are 20% more civilian-held firearms than there are civilians, and gun violence constitutes a public health emergency (Browder 2019).

The implications of WPP are inevitably more profound and severe in the United States than elsewhere. To admire Keanu Reeves as Neo in *The Matrix*, looking cool while he fires an Uzi machine-pistol, is one thing in England or New Zealand, where such weapons are largely unobtainable; quite another in the United States, where an adult can purchase an Uzi with little difficulty. The primary issue for nations which consume American popular culture, but which do not allow ready access to firearms, is more subtle. It is not the make of gun, but the ubiquitous presence of guns which affects perceptions of policing in general and expectations of firearm use in particular.

---

[4] At the time of writing, a tragic mass-shooting has caused to the Canadian government to push for more restrictive gun control laws (Cecco 2020).

7.3   Weapon Product Placement and Scripting

Ray Surette (2016b) argues that "copycat crime", criminal actions inspired by media depictions of crime, is a more common phenomenon than is typically acknowledged. He draws on a range of theoretical approaches from multiple disciplines to explore copycat crime: psychology, the study of diffusion of innovation, social learning, and communication and media studies (Surette 2016a). At the core is the importance and power of imitation in the human psyche: "we are hard wired for imitation" (2016a: 55). Imitation is a key learning tool, the means by which people acquire important knowledge and skills. The most influential models for imitation are family and peers, but media is another key source of modelled behaviours.

Among Surette's points worth emphasising here is the importance of **narrative persuasion**. When people consume media for entertainment or escapism, they are not assessing factual information: rather, they are seeking an enjoyable and interesting story. As a result, factual details are likely to be absorbed with less critical thought (Surette 2016a: 53). This is the great attraction of product placement as a marketing technique, and reinforces the particular effectiveness of more subtle messages. An allied concept is that of **scripting**, pre-established behavioural directions held in the memory (Surette 2016a: 54). Scripts, patterns of behaviour in response to particular situations or stimuli, can be learned through experience and observation of others but also through media (Bushman et al. 2013; Campos 2015). A script is more powerful and more likely to influence real-world behaviour if the actor is unconscious of following it—in other words, if the behaviour seems natural and inevitable.

Surette (2016a) sets out a number of hypotheses about the factors likely to make media more criminogenic (inspiring or encouraging criminal behaviour). These hypotheses are untested, but they are broadly supported by the literature surveyed. Among them are the following:

- "Media crimes shown as successful will be the most criminogenic." (p. 62)
- "Media portrayed crimes that evoke strong emotions will generate more copycat crime than non-emotional generating crimes." (p. 62)
- "Media content that provides …clear, explicit visual content will increase copycat crime rates." (p. 62)
- "Criminal models portrayed as heroic, competent, attractive, admired, high status and instructive, and with positive motives for committing a crime will generate more copycats." (p. 63)
- "General media crime content that neutralizes the negative effects of crime by reducing individual responsibility and distress for crime, reduces the perception of crime harm, condones crime, or shows crime as righteous will increase copying." (p. 63).

Such hypotheses can, we argue, be equally applied to other forms of behaviour. This is uncontroversial in the field of public health. Discussing screen gun violence, Bushman et al. (2013) are blunt:

> Previous research has shown that when exposed to movie characters who smoke, many youth are more likely to start smoking themselves; the same effect is true for characters who drink. Similarly, we predict that youth will be more interested in acquiring and using guns after exposure to gun violence in films.
>
> (Bushman et al. 2013: 1017).

Policing behaviours are qualitatively different from behaviours in the wider population. Police are trained in their craft and subject to supervision and discipline in their execution of it. Formal training and professional experience should over-ride expectations and scripts learnt from popular culture (Broadhurst 2009: 65–67; Rogers 2003). However, the influence of popular culture on policing behaviours cannot be discounted, particularly when scripts involving policing are frequently repeated and then influence public perceptions (Eschholz et al. 2004). Taking Surette's hypotheses above, and replacing "crime" with "police gun violence" produces a new set of hypotheses. Police gun violence is not necessarily criminal, but the recast hypotheses make a powerful case for taking WPP seriously as a factor in shaping policing styles.

- Media portrayed police gun violence shown as being successful will be likely to inspire further police gun violence.
- Media portrayed police gun violence that evokes strong emotions will generate more imitative police gun violence.
- Media content that provides clear, explicit visual content will increase imitative police gun violence rates.
- Police models who use gun violence and are portrayed as heroic, competent, attractive, admired, high status and instructive, and with positive motives for perpetrating gun violence will generate more imitation by other police.
- General media police gun violence content that neutralizes the negative effects of police gun violence by reducing individual responsibility and distress for police gun violence, reduces the perception of police gun violence harm, condones police gun violence, or shows police violence as righteous will increase copying.

It is beyond the scope of this book to test these hypotheses against detailed real-world evidence, but we contend that it is reasonable to suggest that media depictions of police violence, including the use of firearms by police, can influence broader community beliefs about policing. Such an effect would correspond with **cultivation theory**, the premise that persistent and long-term exposure to media content has a small but deeply engrained effect on the "perceptual worlds" of audience members (Alitavoli and Kaveh 2018). In an early exploration, (Gerbner et al. 1980) found that people who watched a large amount of television believed that crime was more prevalent, more violent, more random and more dangerous than was statistically justified (Dowler 2002, 2003). Later studies have confirmed the link, though less conclusively (Dowler and Zawilski 2007). Kort-Butler and Hartshorn (2011) also support the broad truth of cultivation theory in linking media consumption and fear for crime, but emphasise that the picture is both complex and subtle.

Dowler (2002) argues that gun violence on television has a cumulative effect on public attitudes to guns.

On television, both villains and heroes employ guns to achieve their desired goals. More often than not, heroes prevail and villains are defeated. This depiction may lead viewers to believe that guns are necessary for protection and justice … Crime drama is rife with violent images and there are mixed messages about the use of firearms. For instance, villains and criminals employ firearms to terrorise and intimidate "innocent" victims. Conversely, crime fighters use guns to foil crime and defend justice. (Dowler 2002: 238, 243).

(Note that, though written years before the show was created, Dowler's words are an exact description of *The Rookie*).

The model of scripting has obvious implications for police dramas, both with high levels of WPP and where the heroic use of gun violence is a frequent means of resolving a crisis: "The media provide scripts for gun use" (Bushman et al. 2013: 1015). These scripts have the capacity to influence people with aspirations to a career in law enforcement and, more generally, to shape public expectations of police and the role of firearms in policing.

The potential effect of television on public understanding of crime can be seen in what is commonly referred to as "the CSI effect". Named after the many television crime series produced under the "Crime Scene Investigation" (CSI) banner, the effect manifests as unrealistic expectations about the speed, efficiency and accuracy of forensic science techniques (Goodman-Delahunty and Tait 2006; Rhineberger-Dunn et al. 2017). The crime solving officers of the various CSI franchises are almost always able to find whatever forensic evidence is needed to demonstrate definitively the guilt or otherwise of the accused, sometimes using outlandish and improbable techniques. While still the subject of some contention, concern has been expressed about the ways in which the CSI effect can influence criminal processes and public expectations, particularly those of prospective jurors. For example, a belief in the infallibility of DNA as evidence, can mean that time and resources are devoted to obtaining and testing samples for DNA when it may not be necessary (Turney 2010). DNA evidence may also be given too much weight by jurors in prosecutions, leading in some cases to wrongful convictions (Vincent 2010). These concerns relate directly to the way in which crime is solved in television dramas. Put simply, without the CSI shows (or something similar) it is less likely that public expectations would be so clear about the role of forensic evidence in "proving" a criminal case.

There are other distortions in the depiction of police work in popular television dramas. Consistent findings show that television dramas give the impression that police are far more effective in solving serious crimes, and far more likely to use force than is the case in the real world (Soulliere 2003; 2004). This can create unrealistic public expectations of police efficacy (Eschholz et al. 2004). Depictions of crime on television over-emphasise violent crimes, such as murder, rape and robbery, and typically portray offenders as motivated by greed, revenge and/or mental illness (Dowler 2003). In an examination of US television and movie portrayals of policing, Robinson (2020) highlights the role and effect of "copaganda"—whereby fictional dramas can normalise injustice and the use of excessive displays of power and force by police officers. The news media tend to portray police as "heroic, professional crime fighters" (Dowler 2003: 111), while police dramas can be more ambivalent. Policing institutions are often depicted as ineffective because of political interference, incompetent leadership and/or a weak legal system, and it is left to a few remarkable, individual officers who are prepared to take risks and break the rules, to get the job done (Dowler 2003: 120). Eschholz et al. (2004) found that American policing dramas align with and promote a punitive "crime control" understanding of crime and offending. People in public life in the United States periodically invoke fictional scenarios to help justify punitive policies. In 2019, the federal Attorney General, William Barr, announced that the federal government would resume carrying out the death penalty, which had not been enforced since 2003. In justifying this decision, Barr cited the Charles Bronson movie *Death Wish* and the Clint Eastwood *Dirty Harry* series as evidence that "it's satisfying to see justice done" (Weinberger 2019: 12).

Gun manufacturers and their marketing arms certainly believe in cultivation theory, not just through WPP in fictional dramas but also as mediated via television news. Squires (2019) examines the marketing strategies employed by weapons manufacturers in the United States, and the importance to them of military and police contracts. This is not just for the obvious reason—a profitable contract—but also because of the marketing value. Police are in the news constantly, and officers are frequently depicted on television news. During the 1980s, American police services upgraded their weapons from revolvers to semi-automatic pistols. A media report on such an upgrade in New York City commented how "the [old] 0.38 revolver with its wood handle looked like a relic next to the sleek metal 9-mm models, the American-made Smith & Wesson, the German Sig Sauer and the Austrian-made Glock 19" (Squires 2019: 35). Squires suggests that in the American context police firearm contracts function as "endorsements for the much more lucrative civilian market … if police units have them, citizens want them" (Squires 2019: 34–35, 45).

The four jurisdictions examined in this book have much smaller civilian firearms markets than the United States, with particular restrictions on handguns and automatic weapons. However, the police services of these countries still represent a source of profitable contracts, and it is the "sleek metal 9-mm" automatic pistols which were adopted in the US in the early 1990s which have become standard. All four jurisdictions examined in this book, including those where police are not routinely-armed, equip police with Glock 17 and/or Glock 22 automatic pistols.

7.4 Chapter Conclusion

Surette (2015) argues that the result of sustained exposure of audiences to media depictions of crime is a "symbolic reality," an understanding of crime, threat and policing which may have little to do with the reality of lived experience in a particular community. Unreal understandings, however, are real in their consequences: a media-driven symbolic reality can drive public policy changes in every aspect of the criminal justice system, including policing. And the media source does not need to make any claim to truthfulness. Hannibal Lector, a fictional character, looms larger in the public consciousness than any number of real-life murderers; the ruthless "Dirty Harry"

Callahan has been invoked by real-life politicians to justify real-world changes to policing law and policy (Street 2016).

In Chap. 4 we demonstrated the steady increase of militarisation in many police organisations, exemplified by a "colour-in" picture for primary school children showing police with firearms strapped to their thighs. It is not possible to demonstrate a causal link between changing police styles in our four locations, and the dominance over the same decades of American dramas which reflect and propagate the armed tradition of policing. However, that there is a nexus between these two developments is obvious. Weapon Product Placement, like tobacco product placement, cumulatively across many different entertainment media and over a long period of time, justifies and normalises the use of firearms by police, to protect themselves and the community.

Many contemporary fictional crime dramas and movies are presented as a convincing proxy for real life, as "realistic", albeit with constructed characters, storylines and, at times, locations. Across American-made crime and policing dramas, firearms are embedded as an integral part of policing. Guns are worn visibly, and used often. This reflects the perception and reality of American policing. By contrast, the omission of firearms from most UK created crime drama, reflects the relatively minor role that guns play in real life policing. Firearms are not perceived to be an essential (or even a visible) part of routine policing in England and Wales.

The symbolic reality of media and the lived experienced of a community interact and reinforce on many levels and in complex ways. However, as we explored in Chap. 6, in the real world the risk of community harm in England and Wales is no greater than is the case in other jurisdictions examined. Deploying routinely unarmed police does not correlate with lower levels of community or police officer safety.

References

Adler, R. (1999). Here's smoking at you, kid: Has tobacco product placement in the movies really stopped. *Montana Law Review, 60*(2), 243–248.

Ali, C. (2017). *Media localism: The policies of place.* Urbana, Illinois: University of Illinois Press.

Alitavoli, R., & Kaveh, E. (2018). The U.S.media's effect on public's crime expectations: A cycle of cultivation and agenda-setting theory. *Societies 8*(2075–4698), 58.

Alves, T. (2018). 10 awesome New Zealand TV shows to watch. *Culture Trip* (London), 21 Mar.

Australian Communications and Media Authority. (2020). *Content rules for broadcasters.* Canberra: Australian Communications and Media Authority.

Australian Government. (2020). *Supporting Australian stories on our screens: Options paper.* Canberra: Australian Government.

Balasubramanian, S., Karrh, J., & Patwardhan, H. (2006). Audience response to product placements: An integrative framework and future research agenda. *Journal of Advertising, 35,* 115–141.

Booker, C. (2004). *The seven basic plots: Why we tell stories.* London: Continuum.

Broadcasters' Audience Research Board. (2019). *The viewing report: Our annual exploration of the UK's viewing habits.* London: Broadcasters' Audience Research Board.

Broadhurst, R. G. (2009). *Policing in context: An introduction to police work in Australia.* Melbourne: Oxford University Press.

Browder, L. (2019). The gun industry wants to sell your kid an AR-15. In: J. Carlson, H. Shapira & K. A. Goss (Eds.), *Gun studies: Interdisciplinary approaches to politics, policy, and practice*. London: Routledge.

Bushman, B. J., Jamieson, P. E., Weitz, I., et al. (2013). Gun violence trends in movies. *Pediatrics, 132*, 1014.

Campbell, J. (1969). *The hero with a thousand faces*. Novato, CA: Pantheon Books.

Campos, L. P. (2015). Cultural scripting for forever wars. *Transactional Analysis Journal, 45*, 276–288.

Cecco, L. (2020). Trudeau announces Canada is banning assault-style weapons. *The Guardian*, 2 May.

Chen, H., & Wang, Y. (2016). Product placement in top grossing Hollywood movies: 2001–2012. *Journal of Promotion Management, 22*, 835–852.

Claus, S. (2017). Canadian broadcasting policy at issue: From Marconi to Netflix. Canadian Radio, Television and Telecommunications Commission. Available from: https://crtc.gc.ca/eng/acrtc/prx/2017claus.html.

Coombs, J., Bond, L., Van, V., et al. (2011). Below the line: The tobacco industry and youth smoking. *The Australasian Medical Journal, 4*, 655–673.

Cowley, E., & Barron, C. (2008). When product placement goes wrong: The effects of program liking and placement prominence. *Journal of Advertising, 37*, 89–98.

Cummings, K. M., & Proctor, R. N. (2014). The changing public image of smoking in the United States: 1964–2014. *Cancer Epidemiology, Biomarkers and Prevention, 23*, 32–36.

Cummings, M, & Cummings, E. (2014). How accurate is Lone Survivor? *Slate* [online]. Available from: https://slate.com/culture/2014/01/lone-survivor-accuracy-fact-vs-fiction-in-the-mark-wahlberg-and-peter-berg-movie-adaptation-of-marcus-luttrells-memoir.html.

Curtin, M., & Shattuc, J. (2018). *The American television industry*. London: Bloomsbury.

Dowler, K. (2002). Media influence on attitudes toward guns and gun control. *American Journal of Criminal Justice, 26*, 235–247.

Dowler, K. (2003). Media consumption and public attitudes toward crime and justice: The relationship between fear of crime, punitive attitudes, and perceived police effectiveness. *Journal of Criminal Justice and Popular Culture, 10*, 109–126.

Dowler, K., & Zawilski, V. (2007). Public perceptions of police misconduct and discrimination: Examining the impact of media consumption. *Journal of Criminal Justice, 35*, 193–203.

Dunleavy, T., & Joyce, H. (2011). *New Zealand film and television: Institution, industry and cultural change*. Bristol, UK: Intellect Books.

Eagle, L., & Dahl, S. (2018). Product placement in old and new media: Examining the evidence for concern. *Journal of Business Ethics, 147*, 605–618.

Earle, S. (1988). *The devil's right hand. LP copperhead road*. Universal City, CA: Uni Records.

ENP Newswire. (2019). Broadcast and media technology market: skyrocketing growth of streaming and transition away from conventional pay TV grab headlines. *ENP Newswire*. Normans Media Ltd.

Eschholz, S., Mallard, M., & Flynn, S. (2004). Images of prime time justice: A content analysis of 'NYPD Blue and 'Law and Order.' *Journal of Criminal Justice and Popular Culture, 10*, 161–180.

Evans, R. W., Farmer, C., & Saligari, J. (2016). Mental illness and gun violence: Lessons for the United States from Australia and Britain. *Violence and Gender, 3*, 150–156.

Fierman, D. (1999). Where hollywood gets its guns. *Entertainment Weekly, 488*, 49, 6 April.

Finlay, K., Marmurek, H. H. C., & Morton, R. (2005). Priming effects in explicit and implicit memory for textual advertisements. *Applied Psychology: An International Review, 54*, 442–455.

Fuchs, M., S. (2005). Big Tobacco and hollywood: kicking the habit of product placement and on-screen smoking. *Journal of Health Care Law and Policy*, 343.

Gardner, E. (2014). Reese witherspoon film dropout sparks lawsuit against financiers. *Hollywood Reporter*, 19 March. Prometheus Global Media, LLC.

Gerbner, G., Gross, L., Morgan, M., et al. (1980). The "mainstreaming" of America: Violence profile No. 11. *Journal of Communication, 30,* 10–29.

Gilbert, A. (2019). Push, pull, rerun: Television reruns and streaming media. *Television and New Media, 20*(7), 686–701.

Glantz, S., Titus, K., Mitchell, S., et al. (2010). Smoking in top-grossing movies–United States, 1991–2009. *Morbidity and Mortality Weekly Report, 59,* 1014–1017.

Goodman-Delahunty, J. , Tait, D. (2006). DNA and the changing face of justice. *Australian Journal of forensic Sciences 38*, 97–106.

Greenhalgh, E. M., Scollo, M. M., & Winstanley, M. H. (2020). *Tobacco in Australia: facts and issues.* Available at: https://www.tobaccoinaustralia.org.au.

Grzyb, T., Dolinski, D., Kozłowska, A. (2018). Is product placement really worse than traditional commercials? Cognitive load and recalling of advertised brands. *Frontiers in Psychology, 9*, article 1519.

Haag, P. (2016). *The gunning of America: Business and the making of American gun culture.* New York: Basic Books.

Hartley, L. P. (1958). *The go-between.* Harmondsworth: Penguin.

Higson, A., et al. (2015). British cinema, Europe and the global reach for audiences. In I. Bondebjerg (Ed.), *European cinema and television* (pp. 127–150). London: Palgrave Macmillan.

Hilgard, J., Engelhardt, C. R., & Bartholow, B. D. (2016). Brief use of a specific gun in a violent game does not affect attitudes towards that gun. *Royal Society Open Science, 3* (11). https://doi.org/10.1098/rsos.160310.

Hudson, S., & Elliott, C. (2013). Measuring the impact of product placement on children using digital brand integration. *Journal of Food Products Marketing, 19,* 176–200.

Truth Initiative. (2018). *While you were streaming: Tobacco use sees a renormalization in on-demand digital content, diluting progress in broadcast and theaters.* Washington DC: Truth Initiative.

Internet Movie Firearms Database. (2020). *The internet movie firearms database.* Available at: https://www.imfdb.org/wiki/Main_Page

Jacobs, R. N. & McKernan, B. (2008). American television as a global public sphere. *Conference Papers—American Sociological Association*, 1.

Jamieson, P. E., & Romer, D. (2010). Trends in US movie tobacco portrayal since 1950: A historical analysis. *Tobacco Control, 19,* 179–184.

Karniouchina, E. V., Uslay, C., & Erenburg, G. (2011). Do marketing media have life cycles? The case of product placement in movies. *Journal of Marketing, 75,* 27–48.

Keller, T. E., Ju, T. W., Ong, M., et al. (2004). The US national tobacco settlement: The effects of advertising and price changes on cigarette consumption. *Applied Economics, 36,* 1623–1629.

Kort-Butler, L. A., & Hartshorn, K. J. S. (2011). Watching the detectives: Crime programming, fear of crime, and attitudes about the criminal justice system. *The Sociological Quarterly, 52,* 36–55.

Kuhn, K.-A.L., Hume, M., & Love, A. (2010). Examining the covert nature of product placement: Implications for public policy. *Journal of Promotion Management, 16,* 59–79.

Law, S., & Braun-La Tour, K. A. (2003). Product placements: How to measure their impact. In L. J. Shrum (Eds.), *The psychology of entertainment media.* London: Lawrence Erlbaum Associates

Leonardi-Bee, J., Nderi, M., & Britton, J. (2016). Smoking in movies and smoking initiation in adolescents: Systematic review and meta-analysis. *Addiction, 111,* 1750–1763.

Levin, M. (1994). Tobacco firm paid $950,000 to place cigarettes in films: Company paid actors in cash, cars or jewelry in early '80s, memos say: Industry says it has halted practice. *Los Angeles Times,* 19 May.

Lyons, A., McNeill, A., & Britton, J. (2013). Tobacco imagery on prime time UK television. *Tobacco Control, 23,* 257–263.

McKay, H. (2014). How Hollywood helps gun makers sell their guns. *Fox News,* 25 Mar.

McKenzie, E. (2018). Top 10 television programmes 2018. *StopPress,* 5 Dec.

McLaughlin, E. (2005). From reel to ideal: The Blue Lamp and the popular cultural construction of the English 'bobby' . *Crime, Media, Culture, 1,* 11–30.

Netflix Investors. (2020). *Financial statements.* Available at: https://www.netflixinvestor.com/fin ancials/financial-statements/default.aspx

Palmer, B. (1998). When product placement goes horribly, horribly wrong. *Fortune, 138,* 48, 21 Dec.

Parliament of Canada. (2014). *Canadian broadcasting policy.* Ottawa: Library of Parliament (Canada).

Pascoe, R. (2012). Content regulation in Australia : Plus a change. *Communications Law Bulletin, 31,* 11–16.

Pohlmann, S. (2019). *Playing the field: Video games and American studies.* Boston: Walter de Gruyter.

Porter, N. (2019). 2018–19 TV season ratings: 90% of veteran broadcast shows fall. *The Hollywood Reporter,* 23 May.

Quinn, K. (2020). Australian creators fear extension of 'emergency' TV content quotas. *The Age* [Melbourne], 19 Apr.

Rhineberger-Dunn, G., Briggs, S. J., & Rader, N. E. (2017). The CSI effect, DNA discourse, and popular crime dramas. *Social Science Quarterly, 98,* 532–547.

Robinson, R. (2020). *Normalising injustice.* The USC Annenberg Norman Lear Center. Available from: https://hollywood.colorofchange.org/wp-content/uploads/2020/02/Normalizing-Inj ustice_Complete-Report-2.pdf

Rogers, M. D. (2003). Police force—an examination of the use of force, firearms and less-lethal weapons by British police. *Police Journal, 3,* 189–203.

SIG Saur. (2020). *SIG Saur: Never settle.* Available from: https://www.sigsauer.com/company/. Accessed 24 Jan 2020.

Soulliere, D. M. (2003). Prime-time murder: Presentations of murder on popular television justice programs. *Journal of Criminal Justice and Popular Culture, 10,* 12–38.

Soulliere, D. M. (2004). Policing on prime-time: A comparison of television and real-world policing. *American Journal of Criminal Justice, 28,* 215–233.

Squires, P. (2019). Semi-automatics for the people? The marketing of a new kind of man. In J. Carlson, H. Shapira, & K. A. Goss, et al. (Eds.), *Gun studies: Interdisciplinary approaches to politics, policy, and practice.* London: Routledge.

Statista. (2020). Number of Netflix paying streaming subscribers worldwide from 3rd quarter 2011 to 4th quarter 2019. Available at: https://www.statista.com/statistics/250934/quarterly-number-of-netflix-streaming-subscribers-worldwide/

Stockwell, T. F., & Glantz, S. A. (1997). Tobacco use is increasing in popular films. *Tobacco Control, 6,* 282–284.

Street, J. (2016). *Dirty Harry's America : Clint Eastwood, Harry Callahan, and the conservative backlash.* Gainesville: University Press of Florida.

Surette, R. (2015). *Media, crime, and criminal justice : Images, realities, and policies.* Stamford: Cengage Learning.

Surette, R. (2016a). Copycat crime and copycat criminals: concepts and research questions *Journal of Criminal Justice and Popular Culture 18,* 49–78.

Surette, R. (2016b). Measuring copycat crime. *Crime, Media, Culture 12,* 37–64.

Turney, L. (2010). The failure of DNA forensic testing: A case study of the 2009 Australian bushfire disaster. *New Genetics & Society, 29,* 225–240.

Vincent, F. H. R. (2010). *Report: Inquiry into the circumstances that led to the conviction of Mr Farah Abdulkadir Jama.* Melbourne: Victorian Government Printer.

Weinberger, E. (2019). One summer in America. *London Review of Books, 41,* 11–18.

Young, A. (2010). *The scene of violence: Cinema, crime and affect.* Oxon: Routledge.

Chapter 8
Do Police Need Guns?

Abstract In this book we have probed the doctrine of minimum force policing. Is "minimum force" merely an aphorism, a rhetorical position which is vulnerable to challenge? Or can the efficacy of minimum force, for both the community and police themselves, be demonstrated with tested evidence? We have also unpacked the armed tradition of policing, and questioned the frequent, confident assertion that the community will be better protected and that police will be safer if they are routinely armed. Again: is there evidence to support this claim? This chapter draws together our explorations of core theoretical and conceptual elements of police power and use of force, the empirical findings of our comparative study, and the discussion of the subtle influence of media on policing style. Our research findings highlight that the assumptions which support the routine arming of police officers need much more careful consideration and analysis than has previously been applied. There is growing pressure in some currently unarmed jurisdictions to move towards more militarised and routinely armed policing. We implore those advocating for such change, and those tasked with making such a fundamental decision, to think through and test the assumptions made about the need for routinely armed police officers. Put simply, do all police officers actually need guns? We do not claim to provide a comprehensive answer, but we hope to demonstrate that the question is real and important, and that the standard rhetorical justifications for arming police are not supported by clear evidence.

8.1 Concluding Thoughts

Despite the title of this chapter, and indeed of this book, the purpose of our study is not to determine whether police need guns. Of course, police need *access to* firearms. We recognise and accept firearms as a necessary part of policing. The question is whether police need guns in every situation, every time they go out on patrol, and whether police firearms should be ubiquitous and visible.

We are not "anti-firearm," and we are certainly not "anti-police". We recognise that policing is a difficult, dangerous and often thankless job. Our central position is that a professional and disciplined police, empowered to use violence on behalf of the community according to the law, and accountable to an independent judiciary, is essential for the peaceful functioning of modern society. Both authors are involved in educating young people, many of whom aspire to careers in law enforcement. We regard it as an honour to do such work. Our society, its most vulnerable sectors in particular, needs committed and well-trained police.

The capacity to use force is essential for effective policing. However, the way in which police use force profoundly influences the perceptions and expectations of the policed community. Police are expected to intervene to resolve, and ideally to prevent, all manner of troublesome situations. Yet, if police used force in every instance where it might be justified, this would almost certainly alienate many members of the community and expose the, often limited, police resources.

In Chap. 2 we highlight that "police use of force is *potential rather than actual*" (Brodeur 2010: 116). The potential capacity to use force in any given situation, but also *not* to use it, enables police to accommodate the expectation that actual force used will be minimal. This frames our examination of two dichotomous models of police power: the doctrine of minimum force (Chap. 3) and the armed tradition (Chap. 4).

Routinely unarmed police are the bodily incarnation of the minimum force doctrine—police can apply potentially lethal force only by exception and in very specific circumstances. We do not contend that the minimum force doctrine of policing is incompatible with routinely arming police. Indeed, in many routinely-armed jurisdictions, "use of force" operational frameworks sit within an expectation of minimum force. However, the fact of police routinely carrying firearms does represent a particular tone and approach. It places the option of lethal force literally in the hands of all officers. Police firearms training, risk management protocols, organisational procedures, and de-escalation processes are not a focus of this book. We acknowledge that each will affect the operational and situational responses of individual officers, and police organisations more broadly. However, in a general sense, we suggest that ready access to a firearm must exert some influence on the decision-making of officers, and affect how they respond to situations of perceived risk when compared with officers who do not carry a firearm.

One example, which epitomises minimum force policing in a situation of extreme risk, is the response of two police officers following the shooting and stabbing assassination of a British Member of Parliament, Jo Cox, in June 2016. The two West Yorkshire Police officers first on the scene were both unarmed. The incident occurred in a public place. Given the extreme risk posed by the offender and the harm already caused, the officers had no choice but to intervene. One of the officers later commented: "there were people out, kids in the street". The two unarmed officers were able to instruct the still-armed offender to set down his weapons. They restrained him, with minimum fuss and no additional harm, until assistance arrived (BBC 2017).

It is worth reflecting upon the likely outcome if the responding officers had carried firearms. Had the offender not put down his weapons on command, he could have been shot dead. The offender would then not have been psychiatrically assessed, would not have faced trial, and would not have received the proportionate punishment dictated by the criminal law. He would have been, de facto, executed, in a society which does not allow the death penalty.

It might be objected: the unarmed police of West Yorkshire just got lucky. What if the offender *had* used his weapons? The response might be: perhaps it was precisely because the police were unarmed, and the offender knew it, that he lay his weapons down. Which invites further interrogation: had the man known that West Yorkshire Police *were* armed, he would have been less likely to attempt his appalling act of terror. And this exchange could go on, indeed in wider discussions of policing it does go on, ad infinitum.

One reason for such largely unproductive debates—illustrative case study, followed by hypothetical, followed by counter-hypothetical, etc.—is an underlying weakness, in terms of both theory and evidence, of the two major streams of thinking in relation to the use of force by police. For both the minimum force philosophy and the armed tradition of policing, the theoretical and evidentiary base is thin, and largely predicated upon presumption and assertion. This is particularly evident in relation to the expectation that police officers and the community are safer when police routinely carry firearms than when they do not.

That carrying firearms increases safety is generally presented as an unchallengeable truth. In Chap. 4 we quote an Australian police official, addressing New Zealand police officers, expressing incredulity "that you guys don't wear guns on your hips … What is it [your firearm] doing in the boot of your car when you are dealing with a violent offender?" (Police News 2019). Such comments encapsulate the "armed tradition" of policing: the uncritical assumption that police must have immediate access to lethal weapons to be effective. Research is beginning to fill the gaps in our understanding of policing and weapons, but the rationale for arming police remains largely rhetorical and symbolic. Proponents assert that guns are essential to ensure the safety of officers and the security of the wider community. Without immediate access to a gun, police officers are at risk and, as a result, the policed community are placed at greater risk of harm. Guns are, therefore, necessary to enable police officers to undertake their role effectively.

New Zealand and Great Britain are two of only 19 countries which currently do not deploy routinely armed police (University of Sydney 2019). In both jurisdictions, shocking incidents of violence in recent years have led to calls for more armed police and, at times, for all police to be armed. The evolution of police firearms policy in these jurisdictions has been largely reactive. Incidents in which unarmed police have failed to prevent a tragedy, or where lethal violence has been directed towards officers or the community, leads to pressure for increased police access to and deployment of firearms. Conversely, incidents in which armed police kill or seriously wound a non-offender generates concern about police use of guns, and the need for better use of non-lethal alternatives to firearms (Rogers 2003; Waldren 2007). Police may feel safer with ready access to firearms but, as we note in Chap. 4, this may lead officers to expose themselves to more dangerous situations, which can then increase the risk of harm.

Despite the global prevalence of routinely armed police, there has been very little empirical research testing the assumption that they or the communities in which they patrol are safer than those in which police officers do not typically carry firearms. In Chaps. 5 and 6, we build upon historical, theoretical and conceptual discussions, and search for data. Chap. 5 sets out the rationale for our study, and Chap. 6 details the findings of our comparative examination of the correlation between community safety, police officer safety, and the routine arming of police.

We examine four jurisdictions which are broadly comparable, in terms of political and social structure, economic stability, cultural mix and heritage, and prevailing local and global risk. A key difference is whether or not their police are routinely armed: in Canada and Australia they are; in England and Wales, and in New Zealand they are not. We use publicly available data, published documents and media sources to analyse patterns of crime, behaviour and risk, and to explore the relationship between the routine arming of police officers, community and police officer safety. To mitigate the potential effects of geography and national population differences, where possible we repeated our analyses at a city level, comparing one city of similar size and status in each location: Manchester, England and Wales; Toronto, Canada; Brisbane, Australia; Auckland, New Zealand. Our objective was to provide an evidence-based assessment of the doctrine of minimum force and of the armed tradition, by exploring key measures of community and police officer safety within jurisdictions where police are either routinely armed or routinely unarmed. Our analysis considers community safety and police officer safety by comparing key data for each jurisdiction. If the routine arming of police officers does ensure or increase safety, as is so often claimed, then there should be some evidence to support this within the data.

We recognise the limitations of framing our analysis within a binary perspective, of routinely armed or routinely unarmed police. The decision to deploy fatal force, and wider patterns of criminal behaviour are determined by more than the routine presence or absence of a firearm. A complex set of drivers underpin and determine specific and general policing responses, which embody procedural, cultural, situational, political, demographic, and individual officer characteristics. Nevertheless, at a macro level, meaningful comparisons can be made which test core assumptions about the routine presence or absence of a firearm. Rather than determining direct causal relationships, our purpose has been to examine the quantum of risk associated with routinely armed or unarmed police. We have sought to identify correlations between a number of key measures of safety and the presence or absence of police firearms.

Our findings show that homicide levels are broadly comparable across the four jurisdictions, although slightly higher in the two routinely armed locations. For two of the other key crime indicators, assault and rape, there were no notable differences, but robbery was found to be higher in England and Wales than in the other three jurisdictions. The rate of fatal police shootings of civilians is significantly higher in the armed jurisdictions, at both national and city level. Our study shows that the difference in the key crime indicators is not sufficient to explain the far higher number of fatal police shootings in armed jurisdictions. Looking at the more general discharge of police firearms (not necessarily causing a fatality) and the use of conducted energy devices, the data points to lower use in the non-routinely armed jurisdictions. For other measures of police safety, the rate of non-accidental police deaths is higher in routinely armed Canada than routinely unarmed England and Wales. In the cities, the differences were found to be more nuanced.

The key point to emphasise across our analysis, is that **we found a clear and repeated absence of definitive evidence to support the contention that routinely arming police officers inevitably or invariably improves community or police safety**, whether by deterring violent crime, creating a level of reassurance, or through higher levels of effective police intervention. When comparing Canada and England and Wales, the latter jurisdiction is "safer" by all measures except robbery. In England and Wales, homicide levels are lower, and the rate of fatal police shootings is approximately 18 times lower. The findings are less clear-cut for New Zealand and Australia. However, overall, our analysis has found insufficient empirical evidence to support the assumption that routinely arming police officers increases safety.

We also look at civilian deaths caused by police shootings. It is important to stress that we were not able to determine the precise nature of such deaths, or whether any particular shooting was justified. Using overall homicide rates as a broad indicator of the risk of violence, there are no significant differences between the four jurisdictions. Each of the four jurisdictions has an expectation of minimum force in policing. However, the risk to civilians of being shot by police officers is significantly higher in routinely armed Canada than in the other three jurisdictions. Canada, in particular, appears to exemplify the law of the instrument (Horowitz 1962; Kaplan 1964). Australia differs from Canada with respect to key risk indicators, despite also deploying routinely armed officers. It is beyond the scope of this project, but a more detailed comparative examination which includes police firearms training, operational procedures, police and public attitudes to firearms, and the overall effects on police and community safety may offer useful insights into the different levels of risk in these two jurisdictions.

We have been transparent in not attempting to explain the patterns within our data. Given the macro-level statistical approach employed, causal linkages cannot and should not be discerned. However, we contend that our findings provide an empirically-informed challenge to the assumption that the routine presence of armed police increases and ensures community safety and/or police safety. That there are differences within and between the jurisdictions further undermines the notion of a "universal truth" that armed police make us safer. We conclude Chap. 6 by acknowledging that there may be reasons to justify a move towards the routine deployment of armed officers, but an inevitable increase in safety is not one of them.

The findings of our study fall short of demonstrating clear beneficial effects of routinely armed police. This begs an important question, which we attempt to answer in Chap. 7. Why do we hear calls to arm currently unarmed police officers? Why is there such a strong and deeply embedded association between the deployment of police with guns and the assurance and expectation of safety for all? There is no clear, demonstrable advantage, either in terms of community safety or the safety of police, in arming police. At most, where police are not routinely armed the evidence suggests that police themselves are at no greater risk of harm, while the wider community may actually be safer. Absent clear evidence in support, the "common sense" view that arming police is natural and inevitable, an obvious move which cannot be contradicted by any person of good will, is not common sense at all. To explore from where such sentiment arises and how it continues to hold firm, we examine the particular role played by the media.

Many contemporary fictional dramas and movies are presented as a convincing proxy for real life, as "realistic" and so reflecting and with implications for the real world. American-made crime and policing dramas dominate the cultural landscape of Anglophone screen entertainment. These productions depict firearms as an integral and essential part of policing. Guns are worn visibly, and used often. This portrayal reflects the perception and reality of American policing. It is a circular relationship; one reinforcing the other. American media, with its high levels of Weapon Product Placement and embrace of the armed tradition of policing in its plotlines and its imagery, cumulatively and in the long term, influences attitudes and expectations, not just in the United States but across the world.

This influence is difficult to quantify, but it is real. It surely is no coincidence that the jurisdiction where the minimum-force doctrine of policing is strongest, England and Wales, also has the most popular and robust local screen drama industry of the four locations examined in our study. The omission of firearms from most UK created crime drama, reflects the relatively minor role that guns play in real-life British policing. Firearms are not perceived to be an essential (or even a viable) part of routine policing in England and Wales. The symbolic reality of media and the lived experience of a community interact and reinforce on many levels and in complex ways. The increased adoption of the armed tradition of policing in Australia (see Chap. 4) has coincided with American police dramas coming to dominate popular culture in that country. Yet, as we explore in Chap. 6, in the real world the risk of community harm in England and Wales is generally no greater than is the case in the other jurisdictions examined. Deploying routinely unarmed police does not correlate with lower levels of community or police officer safety.

There is no clear, unambiguous evidence that deploying routinely armed police officers increases safety. We accept the many limitations of our current study, but those very limitations are primarily the result of a lacunae at the heart of policing research. No one has previously asked this basic question: do police need guns?

The assumption that police need guns for their own safety and for the safety of the community—nigh universal in jurisdictions where police are routinely-armed, and growing in strength where police are not routinely-armed—lacks any hard evidence to support it. From where, then, does this assumption emanate? It is difficult to avoid the conclusion that this apparently hard-nosed, grim, realistic endorsement of the armed tradition of policing is substantially derived from the fantasies of American scriptwriters.

We do not pretend that this book has done anything more than begin an important conversation. Our hope is that other researchers will look at the experience of policing in many different places, and in a range of ways, to build a body of empirically derived, testable knowledge which can be used to inform police, policy makers and the wider community.

Should police be routinely armed, or not? It is a profound, important question. Like any serious public policy issue, it needs to be examined fully and robustly, considering the best real-world evidence available.

References

BBC. (2017). Jo Cox police given bravery medals for tackling killer, *BBC News*, 16 Nov. Available from: https://www.bbc.com/news/uk-england-42012070. Accessed 30 Apr 2020.

Brodeur, J.-P. (2010). *The policing web.* Oxford: Oxford University Press.

Horowitz, M. J., (1962) Trends in education: report on the annual meeting of the American Educational Research Association (AERA) held on February 19–21 1962. *Journal of Medical Education*, *37* (June):634 [Association of American Medical Colleges, Baltimore, Maryland. USA].

Kaplan, A. (1964). *The conduct of inquiry: Methodology for behavioural science.* San Fransisco: Chandler.

Police News [New Zealand]. (2019). Tactical options high priority. *Police News*, Nov, *12*.

Rogers, M. D. (2003). Police force—an examination of the use of force, firearms and less-lethal weapons by British police. *Police Journal, 3,* 189–203.

University of Sydney. (2019). *GunPolicy.org* [online]. University of Sydney. Available from: https://www.gunpolicy.org/about. Accessed November 30, 2019.

Waldren, M. (2007). The arming of police officers. *Policing: A Journal of Policy and Practice 1*(3), 255–264. https://doi.org/10.1093/police/pam043